WORKING WITH
SOFT FURNISHINGS

Working with Soft Furnishings

A Practical Guide to Professional Techniques

CHARLOTTE DUNKERLEY

WARD LOCK

A WARD LOCK BOOK
First published in the UK 1996
by Ward Lock
Wellington House
125 Strand
LONDON WC2R 0BB

A Cassell Imprint

Copyright Text © Charlotte Dunkerley
1996
Illustrations © Ward Lock 1996

First paperback edition 1998

Distributed in the United States
by Sterling Publishing Co., Inc.
387 Park Avenue South, New York,
NY 10016-8810

A British Library Cataloguing in
Publication Data block for this book
may be obtained from the British
Library

ISBN 0 7063 7735 4

Typeset by BCP Ltd, Welshpool, Powys,
Wales.

Printed and bound in Spain by
Bookprint S. L. Barcelona

FRONTISPIECE: This lavishly trimmed treatment is less complicated than it looks. The gathered 'gothic'-shaped valance has been suspended from a shaped board screwed with 'L' brackets to the top of the pelmet board.

For my children and grandchildren
with love

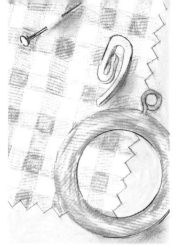

CONTENTS

NOTE

Throughout this book both metric
and imperial measurements are given.
These are not interchangeable, so one
system or the other should be used.
Where accuracy is essential, exact
conversions of the metric
measurements have been made.
Elsewhere the imperial measurements
have been rounded up or down for
convenience.

Unless otherwise indicated, the seam
allowance for each project is
2 cm ($\frac{3}{4}$ in).

INTRODUCTION

If you can sew, you already know more about soft furnishings than you might think you do! Many of the techniques used in dressmaking are the same as those needed for making soft furnishings.

This book is intended not only for people wanting to know how to make soft furnishings for their own homes but also for those thinking of using their sewing skills commercially. When I started my home-based workroom, the conditions were far from ideal – my sewing machine was in one room, the ironing board in another and the sitting-room floor provided the only large flat surface for cutting out fabrics. My productivity was also limited by family commitments.

Although I had always enjoyed sewing and could also draw reasonably well, the prospect of developing these hobbies into a business was quite daunting. I had to learn as I went along and was constantly frustrated by not knowing what standards were expected professionally. Eventually I was able to take a soft furnishing course at a technical college. This proved enormously helpful, not least because of the opportunity of sharing ideas with my fellow course students.

The more you know, the more confidence you will have in dealing with your clients. Read every book and article on soft furnishings and interior decorating that you can find. Learn something about architecture and the decorative arts too.

However experienced you become, you will still be nervous when delivering your work. With large jobs it is like going on stage. As you complete the final touches, stand back and look at everything very critically. Ask yourself if you would be prepared to pay for it. This is a very good yardstick.

Strangely enough, you will tend to forget about your successes and remember only your failures. Try not to agonize over mistakes even if they cost you a lot of time or money to put right. Look on them as lessons well learned and avoid repeating the error. Never allow yourself to wonder if you can get away with something – usually you cannot.

The work is hard but it is also interesting and creative. I hope that this book will enable you to avoid some of the pitfalls I suffered.

▲ A straightforward and stylish look; the choice of fabrics is well suited to the
simple styling of the soft furnishings.

1

THE WORKROOM

Adequate space is essential when making soft furnishings. The room or working area must be large enough to accommodate a very big table and a sewing machine, with space too for storing miscellaneous items tidily.

Do make sure that the lighting is good. Install fluorescent lighting as soon as possible. Winter working hours are extended if the workroom is well-lit. Attach an angle-armed lamp to the sewing machine table so that adjustments to its position can be made easily – it is surprising how often one does hand-sewing while sitting at the machine.

FIRE HAZARDS

Fire is a very real danger in a workroom and every possible precaution must be taken to prevent it. If you have a portable gas or electric heater, a mesh fireguard must always be kept in front of it and the fluff must be removed from the elements regularly.

Do not smoke in the workroom or allow visitors to do so. The smell of smoke also taints the fabrics and takes weeks to disappear. Clients can justifiably be very sensitive about this.

Make a habit of switching the electricity off at the power point on leaving the room even briefly. This is particularly important as far as the iron is concerned. For safety install a wall mounting for the iron and make sure that it is always used.

PROTECTING FABRICS

Do not wear make-up when working. Fabrics can brush against your face picking up a trace of colour; the combination of oils and dyes can prove indelible. Lipstick is particularly hazardous.

Banish felt-tip and ballpoint pens from the room. The dyes are virtually ineradicable.

Bloodstains, caused by pricked fingers, are commonplace but can be successfully removed by dabbing the mark with a scrap of clean fabric moistened with saliva. This must be done before the bloodstain has dried as it is then easier for the enzymes in the saliva to work on the proteins in the blood. Do not, however, use saliva on moire, silk or silky fabrics

Avoid taking drinks into the workroom and never put cups or glasses on the work table, particularly if fabric is laid out on it. Keep the kettle in the kitchen – leaving the room for a few minutes to make a hot drink provides a welcome break.

WORKING CLOTHES

Try to wear clothes that do not retain fluff and threads too readily.

As you will be standing much of the time, it is important to wear comfortable shoes. If the workroom is cold, wear thick socks or boots to keep your feet warm.

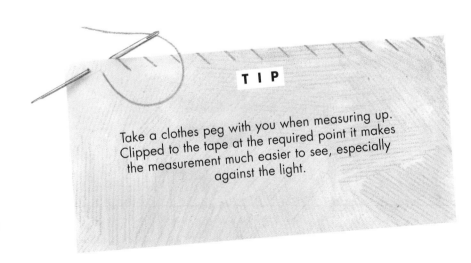

TIP

Take a clothes peg with you when measuring up. Clipped to the tape at the required point it makes the measurement much easier to see, especially against the light.

—— EQUIPMENT ——

SEWING MACHINE

A sewing machine will be, by far, your most important and expensive item of equipment. A domestic machine, provided it is fairly heavy and set into a table, will do in the beginning but domestic machines are not intended to be used for more than four or five hours' sewing a week. When making soft furnishings on a business basis, you will need to invest in a 'professional' machine. Do buy a new one if possible – second-hand machines are usually either worn out or so old-fashioned that they are not versatile enough for your requirements. Your domestic machine can be kept with you when hanging curtains or for doing alterations and repairs on site.

Most of the major manufacturers produce professional/industrial machines and the model you choose is a matter of personal preference. The features for which you should look are given in the checklist.

Because a sewing machine is such an important and expensive purchase, it may be worth talking to your bank manager about a loan to cover the cost. The interest charges will of course increase the cost of the machine so it is wiser to wait until you have saved the necessary money.

Some machines have measuring gauges near the sewing foot which are a useful feature. Strips of adhesive tape marked with various measurements that are needed frequently (such as the one for a standard hand pinch pleat) can be added.

Have the machine serviced at least twice a year and make a ritual of cleaning and oiling it on, say Friday. Try to oil the machine at the end of the working day, leaving a pad of material under the foot to mop up oil. The manual will explain where to oil your particular machine but there is one more place which is not usually shown in manuals: the bobbin casing. Take out the bobbin and using a cotton bud smear the inside of the bobbin casing lightly with oil. Use the highest grade of oil available and make sure that it is white, not yellowish in colour. All-purpose household oil is not suitable.

Change the needle frequently and certainly at the start of each new, big job. The machine will work much better if the needles are sharp. Most, but not all, soft furnishing fabrics are more easily worked using a fairly fine needle (size 12). Many professional/industrial machines use needles which do not have a flat-sided head. All types of machine needle must be inserted into the needle holder so that the long groove exactly faces the direction in which the thread approaches the eye. If it is even a little off the mark, the thread will break frequently and the stitch tension will go awry. Check the angle of the needle eye by adjusting it to the straight with the point of a pin. A blunt needle makes a thumping noise as it stabs into the material; a bent needle damages the inner works; and a needle with a flattened point will pull threads and ruin fabrics.

CHECKLIST

A strong and sturdy table mounting

A really strong motor capable of dealing with at least 15 layers of usual-thickness material at a time

A good selection of sewing feet. Cording feet designed to take the various thickness of piping cord are essential

Automatic bobbin winding

A zigzag stitch facility

Knee-operated foot lifter

Holders for kops of sewing thread

As long and as high an arm as you can find, for dealing with bulky items

A good, adjustable light – you can swap the one on your machine for one with an angle arm – screw it to the table at the back

TABLE

A really large, long and high table is the second most expensive item of equipment but it is essential. The speed and ease with which you work depends upon the table and your health depends on it too! It is very bad for your back, neck and shoulders to work at a surface which is not the proper height for you. Do not even think of cutting out fabric or working on it on the floor as this could trigger back problems.

If possible, the table should be at least 3.5 m (11 ft 6 in) long and double a comfortable stretch in width – this is between 1.5 m (5 ft) and 2 m (6 ft 6 in) depending on the length of your arm. The height depends on your height – a measurement taken from the mid-point between your navel to what is delicately known as the bikini line is just right as this will keep your back straight when working at the table. If the table is too long, time will be wasted by walking around it. If the workroom is large enough, construct some smaller tables to extend the length when needed.

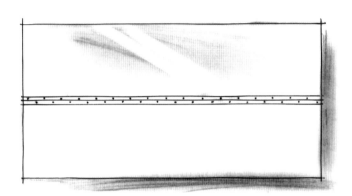

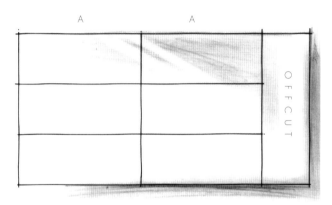

Fig. 1

(a) Cut an MDF board, 1.5 cm (⅝ in) thick, in half down its length to make a portable, temporary table. Use piano hinge to join the pieces.

(b) Make the 'legs' from two more sheets of 1.5 cm (⅝ in) MDF board cut as in the diagram. The sections A and A should be cut to suit your height. One sheet of MDF will make three 'open book' legs. Six 'legs' are needed to support the board. Use a piano hinge to join the legs.

(c) Assemble the legs and the top board to make a table.

A temporary, large table can be made from a sheet of maximum density fibreboard (MDF) resting on piles of books on your dining table. If the board is cut in half down its length, the pieces can be stored more easily, see Fig. 1. Such a table will be wobbly but is better than nothing.

A permanent table should be designed so that it is rigid and also has shelves underneath for storing bolts of linings and interlinings. Fig. 2 illustrates the type of table you should construct. If you and your partner are average handymen, it is not difficult to put a work table together . . . it is not impossible to do single-handed but, because of its size, you are likely to need help. As this is not a table that has to look beautiful, a carpenter is not essential.

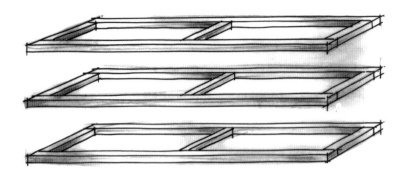

Fig. 2

▲ (a) Make three 'frames' 5 cm (2 in) smaller all round than the table top. Use 4 x 4 cm (1⅝ x 1⅝ in) dressed timber screwed together.

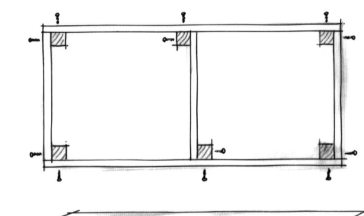

◀ (b) Cut 6 x 6 cm (2⅜ x 2⅜ in) dressed timber for the legs to a height to suit you. Screw the base frame to the bottom of the legs, then cut MDF board to fit the frame with cut-outs for the legs. Repeat for the second shelf.

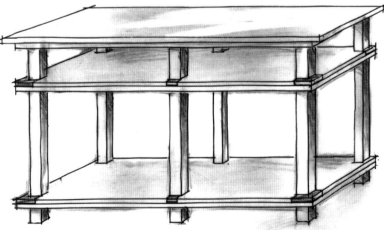

◀ (c) Use a single sheet of 1.5 cm (⅝ in) MDF board (lengthened with a further section if necessary) for the top and screw it down on to the top frame.

TIP

Cut thread on the diagonal as this makes it very much easier to thread the needle, especially the needle of a sewing machine.

Cover the top of the table with curtain lining material (joined offcuts will do), pulling it taut and stapling the material in place under the lip of the table. Shrink the material taut to the table top by spraying it with water and leaving it to dry overnight. Use a marking ink pen to create an 'instant measure' in centimetres and inches down the sides of the table and across the top and bottom. This will save hours of time when measuring fabrics. Replace the cloth covering as and when necessary. It can become remarkably dirty.

STORAGE

Cupboards in a workroom make it look very tidy, but they are not particularly convenient. Shelves in varying lengths and widths keep stocks visible. It is necessary to have some safe place in which to store goods awaiting completion and delivery – on big jobs this can be quite a problem with every available space in the whole house taken over. A cheap worktop from a DIY superstore, raised a little from the floor on bricks, is useful for storing such items.

DRAPING BOARD

This is a full sheet of fibre board soft enough to stick pins into. It is used for draping the templates for swags and, inevitably, for the storage of a lot of small items such as packets of needles and press studs. Fix it to the wall at a comfortable working height, using rawplugs and screws or simply masonry nails with a flat head, in which case a washer is needed under the head

to help to prevent the board from splitting.

CARPET

Close carpeting in a workroom provides warmth and insulation round the feet, but it makes the room much more difficult to clean. Cheap linoleum, varnished floorboards or sealed bricks or tiles are easier to clean. Strips of old carpet round the table can be moved when cleaning the room.

IRON AND IRONING BOARD

Invest in a really good quality steam iron and get the flex professionally modified to lengthen it sufficiently for the iron to reach every part of the table. Try to have the power socket installed at the height of the table and at its midway point.

You will probably generally use the table as an ironing board (cover it with an old blanket clipped down at the corners) and an ironing board will only be useful for small items. Cover a length of 5 x 1.5 cm (2 x ⅜ in) board with unbleached interlining (often called bump if it is very fluffy and loosely woven) and use this to shove down narrow items (such as tubes for put-on frilling) to iron the seams open before turning the tube inside out – much easier and much quicker.

VACUUM CLEANER

This should have a flexible hose if possible. Workrooms get very messy and dusty, so need to be cleaned regularly.

WASTE BIN

A plastic dustbin is ideal. Other receptacles to use near the sewing machine are also needed. Oblong, plastic boxes are ideal. Use one as a waste bin and have three or four more for 'dribble folding' (page 85) bias strip and so on into.

COTTONS AND THREADS

Matching colours are only necessary for stitching which will actually show. White, cream, ecru or grey can be used for most work. Buy the biggest spools of thread which the machine can carry and use pure cotton with a thin twist for nearly everything. Man-made thread, or a mix, is necessary when sewing man-made fibres – the old rule of 'like to like' applies in soft furnishing as it does in dressmaking. The advantage of using pure cotton thread is that it can be ripped if you make a mistake, whereas polyester thread has to be snipped or unpicked because it is so strong that it could otherwise tear holes in fabric. Use mercerized thread for both machining and hand-sewing. Because there is so much fluff in a workroom, unmercerized threads just pick it up and will not, therefore, pull through the fabric easily. Tacking thread is not mercerized.

You will also need spools of much stronger threads such as tatting and crochet cottons for stitching the sides of curtains and many other jobs. Ideally linen thread should be used but it is very expensive and a thickish cotton is a very adequate substitute.

LININGS, INTERLININGS AND HEADING TAPES

MISCELLANEOUS EQUIPMENT

ADHESIVE
A rubber-based adhesive is needed for sticking fabric to pelmet boards.

APRON
I wear a sturdy cook's apron which is long enough and wide enough to meet at the back to cover my skirt or trousers. There are two pockets on the apron: a smallish one on the bib with handy divisions which I use to hold spools of cotton and pencils, and a larger one lower down which I use to hold scissors, measuring tape, seam ripper, scissor sharpener and so on.

Keep a selection of needles, impaled, horizontally, through the top of the bib.

Make a habit of putting the tools straight back into their appropriate pocket as this saves wasting time searching for equipment. When I am hanging curtains, the pockets hold the necessary tools. I find too that putting on my apron at the beginning of the working day and taking it off in the evening has a psychological significance.

BRICKS
You will need at least 10 house bricks covered with material and with a strong handle to carry the considerable

weight, see Fig. 3. Bricks are invaluable anywhere an extra pair of hands is needed.

Alternatively, fill squarish plastic bottles – the ones with integral handles – with dry sand.

BULLDOG CLIPS
Their uses are infinite so build up a collection. Make sure that the spring opens wide enough to 'bite' the thickness of the table, plus the material laid out on it. Professional clips are available but their long handles are easily knocked as one goes round the table and they are expensive. Two to four professional clips should suffice.

Fig. 3

▶ (a) Cover a brick with interlining cobbled into place like a parcel. Make a strong loop, from face fabric, for a handle. Cut a piece of face fabric to fit the top of the brick, plus seam allowances, and tack it down over the top.

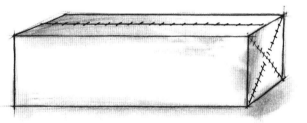

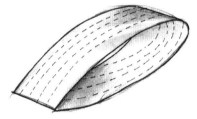

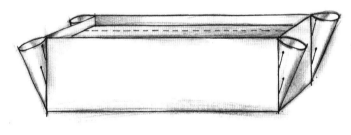

◀ (b) Cut, pin and machine a 'box' to fit the brick, plus a turning in allowance. Turn inside out.

▼ (c) Slip the handle around the covered brick. Fit the 'box' in position and slipstitch it to the top neatly, reinforcing the stitching at the handle for strength.

TIP

If your sewing machine does not have an automatic bobbin winding facility, it saves a lot of time and trouble to load a number of bobbins with thread before starting on a job. Depending on the thickness of the thread a normal bobbin holds about 18 m (19½ yd)

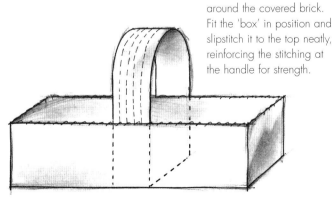

CALCULATOR

A basic one, preferably activated by light.

DOG'S CURRY COMB

This is the easiest way to lift threads and so on from the carpet.

KNITTING NEEDLES

Any old metal needles will do but one should be quite fat and blunt so that it can be used for poking out corners.

MASKING TAPE

Have rolls in 2 cm (¾ in) and 4 cm (1⅜ in) widths. The uses are infinite.

MEASURING TAPES AND RULERS

You will need at least two expanding steel tapes with the capacity to measure upwards of 4 m (13 ft). Make sure that these tapes are marked with both centimetres and inches and that the principal divisions of the measurements are very bold and clear. Boldly marked divisions are very helpful when measuring a window and it is necessary to stand back to assess the possible look of a drop. Buy builders' quality and make sure that the tapes have an easy-to-operate locking mechanism.

You will also need a wooden yardstick (metal ones are too heavy and too slender); two or three fabric tape measures; a 15 cm (6 in) measuring gauge with a moveable pointer; a piece of T-shaped aluminium about 1.5 m (5 ft) long to use instead of a yardstick to draw straight lines from side to side of the fabric; and a T-square with a long arm, though a sheet of newspaper will do just as well.

NEEDLES

Long, thin needles with long eyes are the most useful. I use various sizes of darners and I keep two sizes of curved needle, small and large. The stitching does not have to be as small as that required for dressmaking or embroidery.

NOTEBOOK

Use an A4 hardbacked notebook for writing down measurements, doing drawings and so on. Put your name, address and telephone number inside the front cover so that there is more chance of the book being returned to you should you lose it. When it is full, file it for possible future reference. Do not use scraps of paper for writing down measurements – this looks unprofessional and they are much more likely to be lost. Your notebook is one of your most vital pieces of kit and to lose it is a disaster!

PENCILS, CRAYONS AND CHALKS

Use pencils with soft leads and keep a couple in the top pocket of your apron, You will need a pencil sharpener with two sizes of hole. You will also need tailor's chalk in white and blue, a packet of wax crayons and some blackboard chalk.

PINS

You will need a very large quantity as they have to be replaced frequently. Use the long, fine variety with glass or pearly heads because they are easier to pick up if they fall on the floor and they are also thin enough not to damage the densely woven fabrics of which soft furnishings are so often made. You will also need a very large number of longer, stronger pins of the same type, to use for draping board work. Both types are available in haberdashery departments. If a glass-headed pin becomes accidentally sewn into your fabric just smash the head with a hammer and work it out of the fabric via the point.

Keep some pins in a shallow container anchored to the sewing machine table with a Velcro hook and loop.

TIP

Put a reel of cotton in the top pocket of your apron. Thread it through the pocket and pull off lengths as needed. This saves hours of time!

POWDER DRY-CLEAN SPRAY

This is useful for removing oil-based marks.

'RAKES'

This is my name for the lengths of thick cardboard which I use to mark fabrics for cutting bias and straight strips. Mark and cut in as many sizes as needed, see Fig. 4.

ROLLS OF PAPER

Buy a smooth type of the most inexpensive wallpaper and use the unpatterned side to make templates and patterns. Alternatively, use wall lining paper or vinyl wallpaper.

SCISSORS

You will need large shears, standard dressmaking scissors, small, pointed scissors for snipping and a small, round-ended pair. Do not use scissors that do not have properly moulded

handles and be sure to buy those which are fairly light because a full day spent cutting can make your wrist ache. Sharpen scissors regularly, using the special gadget which is made for the purpose (available from haberdashers).

SEAM RIPPERS

Make sure that these are the big, sturdy kind. The little ones are too small to be useful in a workroom.

SPRAY STARCH

Use to restore stiffness and shine to glazed cottons. Do not forget to cost this in on large jobs using glazed cottons.

STAPLE GUN

This piece of equipment has many uses in making soft furnishings; for example, for suspending swags from a pelmet board. They are obtainable from hardware and DIY supply shops.

STICKING-PLASTERS

Keep the box easily accessible for first aid.

TEMPLATES

Cut out in paper or card and keep to use every time a particular shape is required. Use vinyl wallpaper as it is more durable for patterns that will be used frequently.

You will also need strips of card to use as guides for the hems and turnings on curtains (page 50).

'3M' MICROPORE ADHESIVE TAPE

Available in 1.5–2 cm (⅝–¾ in) widths from chemists.

Fig. 4

▼ Use the 'rake' by placing the base of the card to a straight cut line, or pencil line, and use the straight of the notches to mark the measurements. Standard piping cord, for example, needs crossway strip cut to a width of 5.5 cm (2⅛ in).

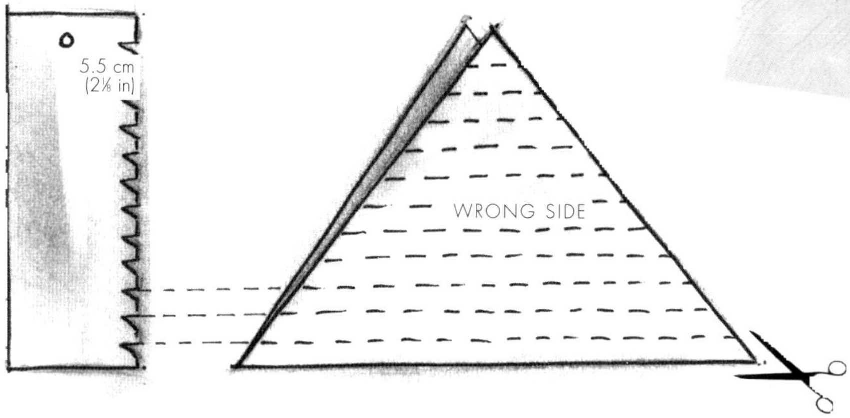

5.5 cm
(2⅛ in)

WRONG SIDE

TIP

Thread the needle before pulling the required length from the spool, then knot the cut end away from the already threaded needle. You will have fewer problems with the thread twisting and knotting back on itself as you sew. This is because the twist of the thread is flowing in the right direction.

2

FURNISHING
FABRICS

The disadvantages of being an agent for furnishing face fabrics outweigh the potential profits unless one has a shop or showroom. The cost of the sample books can be very high, tying up capital for possibly a long time without any sales being made. The big manufacturers are also reluctant to appoint agents unless annual sales above a certain sum are guaranteed. You will, however, make substantial savings by buying linings, interlinings, heading tapes and so on wholesale and you will also save time. These items are charged to the client at retail prices, discovered by checking occasionally in the shops. References are needed to open an account with a wholesaler but the conditions vary, so you have to ask what these are. Always ask your clients for a cash advance to cover the cost of these items and do not start work until you receive it. Equally, do not start work until all the materials required for a job are assembled.

Alternatively, interior decorators often supply bolts of lining and interlining to be used on their behalf. The advantage to you is that your money is not tied up. Label the materials that belong to them with their name and keep a record, attached to the item, of how much you used, for whom and for what, and the date.

I have sample books of plain coloured and patterned linings, interlinings and simple trimmings.

Some are supplied free by my wholesalers, others I have to buy.

Fabrics change colour when viewed in artificial light. Check the colours for matching and suitability in both daylight and electric light.

Many fabrics are a mixture of man-made and natural fibres and it is hard to tell the fibre content if the material is delivered without a detailed label. A simple 'burn test' will give some useful information. Set fire to a snippet of the fabric on an old dinner plate. If the resulting ash is soft and crumbly, the fibre content is natural. If the ash is sharp with black, tarry residues, the material is man-made. If it is a mixture of the two, the fabric is a blend.

Most furnishing materials come in widths of roughly 120–22 cm (47¼–48 in) and 137–40 cm (54–55³⁄₁₆ in) with linings made to the same widths. When making curtains, the width of the lining should be matched to the width of the face fabric so that the seams lie, as far as possible, on top of one another.

INTERLININGS

Interlinings come in varying weights and thicknesses, and are of varying fibre content. The old rule of 'like to like' holds here and a pure cotton interlining should be used with a pure cotton face fabric and a man-made fibre interlining (such as acrylic) with a

man-made fibre face fabric (such as dupion).

Interlinings can be very roughly woven and unbleached. Such an interlining would be suitable used with a thick, heavy face fabric but it would look appalling were it used with a thin face fabric in a pale colour. The colour and faults of the unbleached interlining (bump) will show through the face fabric and alter the colour of the curtains when they are seen against the light from the window. Bleached interlinings are slightly more expensive than unbleached. It is really only a very large workroom or factory which can afford to keep supplies of interlining to meet every contingency. For jobs which require a special interlining, or lining, the necessary amount can be ordered from a wholesaler. What is called a 'cut fee' is charged for it. This makes it a little more expensive per metre (yard) but still cheaper than keeping a whole bolt on hand.

The weight of interlining needed for a particular job will depend on several factors: the height and width of the window; how draught-proof, or otherwise, the window is; what face fabric is being used; and how much space is available to push the curtains back into when they are open. This space is known as 'stack back'. On a tiny window, for instance, it would be ridiculous to use a very thick interlining, but a lightweight one, which is like flannel and called Domette, would be fine. Thin face fabrics, such as silk, can be made to look sumptuous by using a really thick and soft interlining.

I once weighed a pair of 'standard' curtains – three widths of materials with a length of 2.8 m (3 yd) – and they weighed about 15 kg (33 lb). So the strength of the wall and the track must also be considered because of the heavy weight that is going to be suspended. If you are working for an interior decorator, these decisions should be his or hers, and if you are uncertain about what you should use, you have every right to ask.

An interlining which has one side smooth and the other side fluffy should be used with the fluffy side to the wrong side of the face fabric. This is because they will 'felt' together just slightly and this is desirable.

LININGS

The quality of linings varies tremendously. The cheaper they are, the more likely they are to have polyester or viscose as part of the fibre content. Cheap linings are often over-starched, which makes them feel good to start with, but they will sag and bag quite quickly. Sometimes the weave is askew which makes them difficult to handle.

Linings come in 'natural' colours such as white, cream and ecru and also in a wide range of stronger colours and patterns which can much enhance the look of the outside of the house. The dyes in coloured linings, however, can be rather fugitive.

Do not forget the uses of thermal linings to reduce heat at a window, and blackout and rubberized linings for the rooms of small children. Thermal linings such as rubberized ones are not suitable for use in damp atmospheres such as bathrooms and kitchens

because condensation builds up on the wall area behind the curtains.

Most lining fabrics are wound on to the bolt with the length of the material folded in half. It is useful to know that the right side of the lining is to the outside of the bolt. Do not unfold it before cutting your lengths because, with each length placed on top of the next you get an automatic 'right side to right side' for the machining together of the lengths (see pages 42–43).

FACE FABRICS

The patterns, colours, designs and fibre content of face fabrics are as varied as the world is wide! Gradually you will learn which manufacturers produce reliable, well printed, well woven material. You will also learn the others and to groan when their product is delivered to your door.

Like other soft furnishing fabrics the widths are usually 120–22 cm (47¼–48 in) to 137–40 cm (54–55³⁄₁₆ in).

On rolls of face fabric the right side is usually to the inside.

Dress fabrics are not suitable for the making of soft furnishings. The weaves, density and widths are different from furnishing fabrics.

PATTERN REPEATS

All patterned fabrics, whether woven or printed, are designed on about half a dozen basic grids, on which the pattern repeats are based (see Fig. 5).

Only the half-drop – see Fig. 5 (f) – causes any problems in estimating the fabric quantity or in making up. If you do not know how to recognize a half-drop repeat, you will get into dire trouble and expense as a result. Sometimes the fact that the material has a half drop is not mentioned by the salesman to the client or it is not noted on the tag. Sometimes it will be noted simply as 'Patt. Rpt. 27 cm

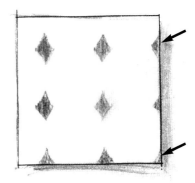

△ (b) Block

Basic pattern repeat grids:

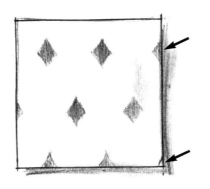

△ (a) Counter change

Fig. 5

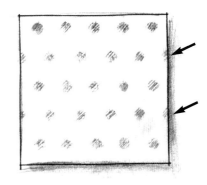

△ (c) Brick

(10⅝ in) HD'. The HD denotes the half-drop. The pattern in the half-drop moves downwards on the fabric so that it is higher on one side than on the other. For cutting fabric with a half drop pattern, see page 41.

Sometimes patterned fabrics have repeat marks printed down the selvage edges but these are not reliable. Always cut lengths of fabric by matching pattern to pattern to ensure that they match.

▲ (d) Diamond

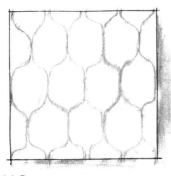

▲ (e) Ogee

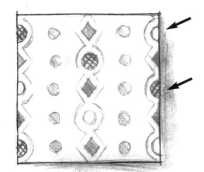

▲ (f) Half-drop

HEADING TAPES, HEADING BUCKRAMS, HOOKS AND WEIGHTS

Curtain tracks and heading tapes are designed to be compatible with one another. The pockets on the tapes line up with the holes of the gliders on the tracks to give a positioning which is either 'on line' or 'underslung'. The tapes available to the trade are often multi-pocket, with the pockets made from separate strands of strong threads so that the hooks can be inserted to an exact point of adjustment. Wholesalers stock a wide range of these products and you will soon discover which suit your work and market best. In general, look for a heading tape with enough body to be reasonably stiff and with cords that are quite thick and strong. It is most annoying if the cord breaks when you are pulling up the heading tape. The cords should also be 'rough'

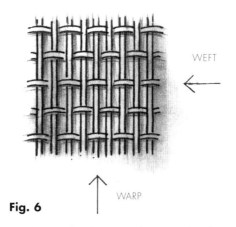

WEFT

WARP

Fig. 6

▲ Showing the directions of warp and weft threads in woven fabric.

enough not to allow the heading pleats to slide about too much.

You will probably use only a limited range of tapes despite the very wide variety which are available.

The pretty, new tapes which pull up to create all sorts of smocked, boxed and clustered headings will appeal to only a few of your clients so you are likely to make these special headings by hand.

Most manufacturers make tapes in both wide and narrow versions. When it is necessary to have a very narrow pelmet, use a narrow heading tape to ensure that the heading is concealed. The wider tapes tend to be heavy duty while the narrower ones are for lightweight work.

The recent introduction of tapes with integral Velcro is a real boon to the making and hanging of pelmets, saving hours of time which used to be spent sewing strips of Velcro on by hand. These tapes are sold under various trade names and are stuck to the front of a pelmet board in combination with adhesive hook Velcro.

DETACHABLE LINING HEADING TAPE
This tape has a double flange at the base into which the raw edge of the top of the lining can be inserted and machined in place from side to side. The tape also has slits which enable it to be suspended from the same hooks as are being used to suspend the curtain.

WARNING

It is essential to comply with the current regulations concerning the necessity of using only fire-resistant fabrics for soft furnishings. Such legislation is subject to amendment and you must check with your local trading standards authority as to your responsibilities as the maker of soft furnishings. If a fire was found to have been caused as a result of your not having used approved fabrics, you could be held responsible.

INTEGRAL RING TAPE

This ingenious tape is used for both Austrian and Roman blinds and, by pulling on the string, it becomes a very neat tape for festoon blinds. The disadvantages lie in the extreme care needed to sew the tape on absolutely straight so that the weft/warp of the tape does not conflict with the weft/warp of the face fabric and lining, and the fact that there are several lines of double stitching down the face of the blind. This is not attractive and it is better to sew on all the rings by hand.

HEADING BUCKRAMS

Used for making hand-headed curtains, these come in three widths: 10 cm (4 in), 12.5 cm (5 in) and 15 cm (6 in). There are two types: those made of simple, lightweight, white, heavily starched loose-weave sheeting and those made of the same basic material but treated with a heat-soluble glue to make them 'fusible'. Fusible buckram is positioned under the top fold of the face fabric of a curtain and ironed in place to hold it in position. Like Velcro, fusible buckram has revolutionized the making of hand-headings. The width of the heading buckram should be adjusted according to the proportions of the curtain you are making.

BUCKRAM

This is very heavily starched sacking or hessian. It has many applications and uses. You should buy 'double starched' buckram because, when moistened, it will become sticky and can be used like fusible buckram. It is available in various widths from 30 cm (12 in) to 92 cm (36 inches) and also in various colours – be careful because the dye can run when the material is moistened. The main use for buckram is for making tie backs and pelmet bands but is not suitable for making hard pelmets.

VELCRO

This wonderful product has totally revolutionized all our lives. Space ships are lined with loop velcro fabric so that articles can be prevented from floating about in the weightlessness of anti-gravity. Velcro is very expensive, so buy it wholesale. It is sold on separate reels for the hook and loop components. It is made in various colours and widths as well as in a self-adhesive version. You will find 2–2.5 cm (¾–1 in) sufficient for most purposes. If the item you are suspending is particularly heavy, the adhesive hook velcro on the pelmet board will have to be reinforced with diagonally gunned-in staples. A few brass panel pins can then be hammered in through the face fabric in such a way that they are hidden and do as little damage as possible (see hanging Hard Pelmets, page 82).

PIPE INSULATION

It will surprise you to see this listed here but it is ideal for stuffing hand-made goblet pleats. It is very firm and lightweight. Try to find it in white rather than grey and buy a good supply. It is made in various diameters so use whichever size is proportionally correct for the relevant article. It can be cut down to make the circumference narrower if necessary.

HOOKS

There is a wide variety of hooks and each manufacturer of heading tape also makes compatible hooks. You do not have to worry about this too much because the difference in size is minimal and you can interchange tapes and hooks without getting into too much trouble. Some hooks are easier to insert and remove than others depending on their design and finish – those with a flat shield at the back are difficult to remove.

Hooks are made from plastic, nylon and metal. Nylon is the strongest for general use with plastic gliders and metal hooks should be used with metal gliders. It is, however, perfectly possible to use metal hooks with plastic gliders but it is not wise to use plastic or nylon hooks with metal gliders because the hooks can be cut through, quite quickly, by the weight of the curtain.

Hand-headed curtains need to be suspended with pin hooks or sewn-on brass hooks. The former are more than adequate for general work though you may need the latter if the curtains are unusually heavy or if your client particularly wants sewn-on hooks (see page 69).

WEIGHTS

These are usually round and look like crude lead buttons. They are quite expensive when bought retail so try to buy them wholesale. Weights of 2.5 cm (1 in) diameter will cater for most contingencies, with two or three extra weights used in one place if necessary – for example, where a seam might pucker without a heavier weight at its base. Positioning depends on the type of curtain and this is described in the relevant instructions.

The type of weight which looks like a string of tiny sausages is intended for use in the gully of the fold of the hem. It must be secured frequently along its length to prevent it from snaking back on itself and taking the corners of the hem back with it.

Short lengths of this leaded tape are useful as weights in sheer curtains.

TIP

The chosen face fabric, lining and interlining should all be laid together, as though they were already a curtain, and held up to the light of a window. This will give you a good indication as to whether or not the fabrics are compatible.

3
How To
Start a Job

Sometimes potential clients may ask you to make some curtains from fabric they have already bought, blithely assuring you that there is no need for you to visit their house to measure up as all the necessary measurements have been taken. Since accurate measurements are essential, it would be extremely unwise to undertake such a job! Never believe other people's measurements is a sound principle.

The style of curtains depends on the window at which they are to be hung and the type of track, pelmet board or rod from which they can be most suitably suspended. The room and its contents and the construction of the wall will help you to decide what is best.

Try to find a competent track fitter (your wholesaler, if you deal with one, may be able to put you in touch with one in your area) because, if the job includes the installation of tracks, his or her advice will be invaluable. Gradually, by studying the catalogues supplied by your wholesaler, you will learn what sort of track treatment will be suitable for a particular job. Usually it is a question of choosing a track that will be strong enough to carry the weight of the curtain fabrics. If you are doing the work for an interior decorator, he or she will have already decided this. For your own, private clients, however you will need to be able to give them advice about tracks

and poles, and also be able to recommend a trackfitter to do the work. In return, the fitter will put work your way.

Make a collection of photographs from magazines showing different ideas and treatments which you think you can copy, or which outline solutions to problems. Mount the photographs on sheets of bond paper using spray glue,

▼ These curtains have been cased on to a pole – an easy form of heading a curtain – but this of course means they cannot be drawn.

and take them with you when discussing a project with a client. Many people are fairly inarticulate when it comes to describing what they want and, also, cannot draw, so these photographs can be very helpful. You should also take pictures of tracks and poles, a few samples of linings and interlinings, your notebook, an expanding steel measuring tape (with the clothes peg for a marker!), a square of carpet to help with getting an accurate measurement if carpet is planned but not yet installed, and a pencil. On massive jobs it is a good idea to have some big self-adhesive labels marked with a number or letter to identify the window and to take a photograph with a simple flash camera. This is a very neat way of jogging your memory later on.

Clients sometimes dream up schemes and choose fabrics which simply will not work in the given location – for example, Austrian blinds in a huge print at a tiny cottage window. It is up to you to acquire the knowledge and experience to be able to give your clients sensible advice – and then help them as tactfully as possible to change their minds. Discuss the styling and the method of construction as minutely as you can and confirm it all in a descriptive form when you send your estimate.

You can take measurements for fabric estimating before the tracks are actually installed but do not head the curtains until you, or your track fitter, have been able to take actual measurements from the installed track – particularly if you are making curtains with handmade headings.

This may mean two trips to the client's home, but it is worth it to make sure that the finished curtains are the right length.

Remember to take into consideration how any treatment will look from the *outside* of the house. Low windows near to a garden path can display the tracking and the linings in close-up to a passer-by. Such linings look most attractive if they have a lightly printed pattern on them – say, a fine stripe or dot – but do remember that a coloured lining can change the colour of the face fabric when it is seen against the light from the inside of the window.

Remember, too, that 'disguising' the window by raising the height of the track or increasing its width, can often enhance the proportions of a

Fig. 7

▼ (a) A small window given a standard treatment.

◀ (b) The same window disguised by raising the pelmet board and using a curved pelmet valance and floor-length curtains.

room enormously. A small window can be made to look much larger and more interesting in this way.

After you have had an in-depth discussion with your client, ask him or her to leave you alone while you take measurements. Clients can be very distracting. If you are measuring up for fabric estimating only, make a note to that effect in your book. Test the walls and ceiling for sound as the noise they make will give you a good indication as

to how strong they are and the sort of fixing which will be needed – the track fitter will find this information very helpful.

Make a little sketch of the window and how it is placed in its surrounding wall with measurements and a note of any hazards about which you will need to know before cutting the material. Sometimes the space above the window (the 'dead light') is non-existent and this will have a bearing on how you are

going to hang the treatment eventually. Swags and tails, for instance, have in most cases to be hung over the edge of a pelmet board and it is easy to install these, if there is a deep dead light area; otherwise the whole pelmet board and track will have to be taken down, the swags stapled into place, and then everything replaced. This is a job which will need two people so you have to be aware of it in advance so that you can include the relevant wages in your estimate.

MEASURING UP

Curtains are made up to be hung so that the tops are underslung, as in the case of poles, or on line with the top of the track or the top of a fascia board (page 133).

For curtains which will be hung from a standard track (one with gliders, a cross-over arm and a pulley mechanism), the measurement is from

the top of the track down to the required point. See Fig. 8 (a).

For underslung curtains which will be hung from a ring on a pole or underneath the baseline of a standard track, the measurement is downwards from the *base* of the large ring or the underside of the track. See Figs. 8 (b) and (c).

For curtains which will be hung from

a fascia board, the measurement is from just above the top of the fascia down to the required point, see Fig. 8 (d), with a *second measurement* taken from the top of the fascia board down to the eye of the glider below it. This is to ensure that you have enough heading standing up above the hook to cover the fascia board when the curtains are closed.

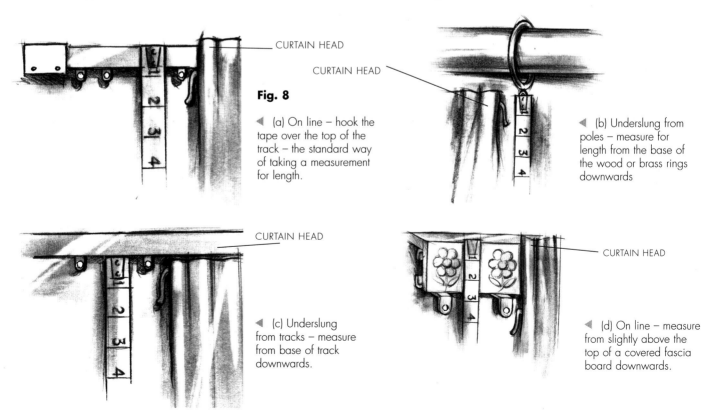

CURTAIN HEAD

CURTAIN HEAD

Fig. 8

◀ (a) On line – hook the tape over the top of the track – the standard way of taking a measurement for length.

◀ (b) Underslung from poles – measure for length from the base of the wood or brass rings downwards

CURTAIN HEAD

CURTAIN HEAD

◀ (c) Underslung from tracks – measure from base of track downwards.

◀ (d) On line – measure from slightly above the top of a covered fascia board downwards.

A measurement from the glider eye or the base of a ring on a pole is called a hook drop. The curtain hook should be inserted so that its top will give you the required drop. If the curtains are not to be underslung, you will also need to know how high the 'stand up' above the tape pocket is required to be to achieve a top line which is on line with the top of the track.

Clients sometimes want their curtains to be over-long – if so, you do not have to be quite so fussy about the length. To be over-long by 5 cm (2 in) is usually quite sufficient. More than this makes the curtains unmanageable and the drag is too much for the cording mechanism. Very over-long is only acceptable for curtains which are not going to be pulled open or shut, but just hang there static and looking decorative . . . Americans call this a 'dead drop'.

Curtains that are going to be installed in an uncarpeted room – for example, a kitchen – should be made slightly shorter than usual to protect the hems from the dust and dirt which accumulates on the floor.

Curtains which are to be installed above a work surface in a kitchen or a vanity unit in a bathroom should be made to be 5–8 cm (2–3 in) above the surface to prevent them getting wet.

▶ These simple curtains have been designed as 'dead drops'. They cannot be drawn open or closed so would therefore be unsuitable for some windows.

Short curtains look best if they reach about 5 cm (2 in) below the window-sill.

Remember to look at the window from the side. It may be necessary to have a wide pelmet board to accommodate a radiator or shutters, for instance. If this is the case, the pelmet board will have to be 10 cm (4 in) wider than such an object. Curtains must be suspended sufficiently far away from the window glass for the lining not to touch the glass as condensation often builds up and this will rot the lining fabric.

Measure up every window in the room separately. There can be differences of height and width even if they look the same at first glance. In houses where two rooms have been knocked together this is an obvious hazard. Do not assume that the measurements in a room in, say, a show house will be exactly the same in the house your client has bought. Builders do not necessarily apply the same thickness of plaster or put the windows in at uniform heights.

▷ All the frills are contrast-bound with a strong red which gives interest and definition to the delicate pattern of the main fabric.

The measurements for the length of the curtains should be taken from both the right-hand side and the left-hand side of the track. If there is a difference, it means that either the track has not been installed level or the floor is not level. If the former, the fault will have to be rectified. If the latter, there is not much you can do to compensate because a curtain which is made and shaped to fit an uneven floor will look fine when it is closed but it will 'stack back' unevenly. As the track *must* be installed on the level (so that the curtains will pull properly), you could try to persuade your client to have the curtains over-long since this will help to disguise the uneven floor. Equally, a plain fabric or a small all-over design will help to hide the problem.

◁ The small size of this window has been disguised with generous long curtains and a gathered pelmet valance.

▶ This checklist contains various points to resolve when visiting a client. Many of the questions are equally applicable when making curtains for your own home.

Measure for the width from end to end of the track if it is already installed and also measure both the length and the width of the pelmet board. Tracks on a pelmet board should be slightly shorter than the board so that the curtains can be turned back towards the wall to stop light showing at the sides. This kind of turn-back is called the return – a word which crops up very, very frequently in this work.

For elaborate jobs you should take very careful measurements of the whole wall, or walls, noting all the different features which may prove to be relevant later on when you are making up the materials. Make copious notes of everything you can think of as there is often a delay of months between your visit to the client and the arrival of the fabrics. In the meantime he or she may come back to you asking questions which you will not be able to answer without such a record.

You will need all the above information, and more, to work out and compose the estimate properly. Taking measurements and talking through the project is time-consuming and therefore costs you money. In certain circumstances you are entitled to ask for a consultation fee and reimbursement of your travelling expenses, for instance, if the interior decorator cannot, or will not, do his or her own fabric estimates. You cannot charge for an estimate for a straightforward, smallish job, but you can mention that there will be a fee for measuring up and estimating for a very big project as the task can take days.

CHECKLIST

In which direction do the windows or French doors open? This will affect the choice of styling for the pelmet or make it impossible to have one at all.

How is everything going to be suspended? What is the condition of the walls or ceiling?

Can the look of the room be improved by disguising the shape of the window?

What is the preferred style?

Are the goods to be lined-only or interlined?

What is the client's preference as to length? Just above the floor or over-long?

Has the fabric already been chosen? What is the width and pattern repeat?

What type of heading for the curtains? Commercial heading tape or handmade headings?

Are there to be tie-backs? What style?

Are there to be extra trimmings such as frilling, contrast binding or piping?

Are there to be trimmings such as rope, braid, fringe or fan edging?

Suggest roller blinds if the face fabric is very sensitive to light. Without protection from direct sunlight silk will rot to shreds within two years.

Suggest net curtains if the windows are very exposed or the interior of the room is visible from the street.

Suggest coloured, thermal or light-proof linings if the window or the use of the room calls for it.

Is there a deadline for the delivery of the made-up goods?

Is the client willing to let you have an advance to cover the cost of material?

Will it be necessary to call in a professional track fitter to supply and install the suspension?

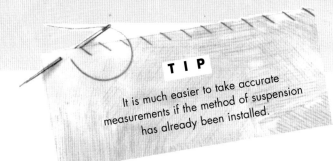

TIP

It is much easier to take accurate measurements if the method of suspension has already been installed.

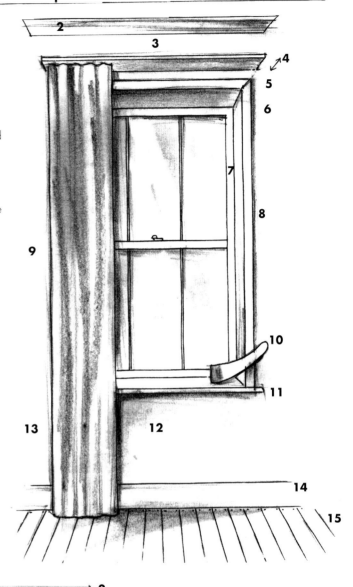

Fig. 9

▶ Identifying words describing the different parts of a window, its surrounds and curtain-making terms:

1 Ceiling

2 Cornice, coving or moulding

3 The area between the top of the window and the ceiling is called 'dead light'

4 'Return' – the depth of the pelmet board from front to back

5 'Soffit' – the upper part of the reveal

6 'Reveal' – the vertical side of the window between the front of the wall and the frame

7 Window frame

8 'Architrave' – moulding around the window

9 'Stack back' – the space taken up by the curtain when it is open

10 'Embrace' – the length of a tie-back

11 Window-sill

12 'Leading edge' of curtain

13 Window edge of curtain

14 Skirting board

15 Floor

Fig. 10

▽ A standard pelmet board and its component parts:

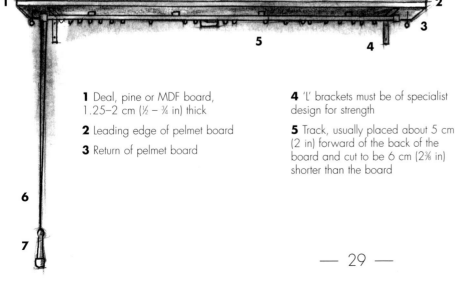

1 Deal, pine or MDF board, 1.25–2 cm (½ – ¾ in) thick

2 Leading edge of pelmet board

3 Return of pelmet board

4 'L' brackets must be of specialist design for strength

5 Track, usually placed about 5 cm (2 in) forward of the back of the board and cut to be 6 cm (2⅜ in) shorter than the board

6 Pulley cord for opening and closing curtains. Specify right- or left-hand draw when ordering

7 Sprung cord tensioner – installed to be hidden behind curtain

Fig. 11

▶ (a) A sample of the type of notes to take when measuring up.

▼ (b) On big, elaborate projects it is worth taking careful measurements of each wall and placing these measurements around a plan of the floor. The measurements denoted by the encircled numbers on the plan are listed below.

1	3.32 m (130²³⁄₃₂ in)	**12**	2.98 m (117¹¹⁄₃₂ in)
2	3.12 m (122⅞ in)	**13**	40 cm (15¾ in)
3	2.20 m (81⅝ in)	**14**	38.5 cm (15⁵⁄₃₂ in)
4	1.78 m (70¹⁄₁₆ in)	**15**	94 cm (37 in)
5	1.80 m (70⅞ in)	**16**	2.84 m (111¹³⁄₁₆ in)
6	70 cm (27⁹⁄₁₆ in)	**17**	39 cm (15¹¹⁄₃₂ in)
7	52 cm (20⁷⁄₁₆ in)	**18**	56 cm (22¹⁄₃₂ in)
8	42 cm (16¹⁷⁄₃₂ in)	**19**	3.09 m (121²¹⁄₃₂ in)
9	10 cm (3¹⁵⁄₁₆ in)	**20**	815 m (268¹¹⁄₃₂ in)
10	1.05 m (40¹¹⁄₃₂ in)	**21**	4.40 m (173¼ in)
11	1.90 m (74¹³⁄₁₆ in)	**22**	15 cm (522⁹⁄₃₂ in)

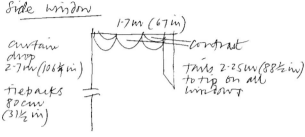

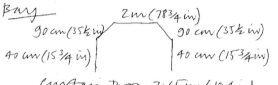

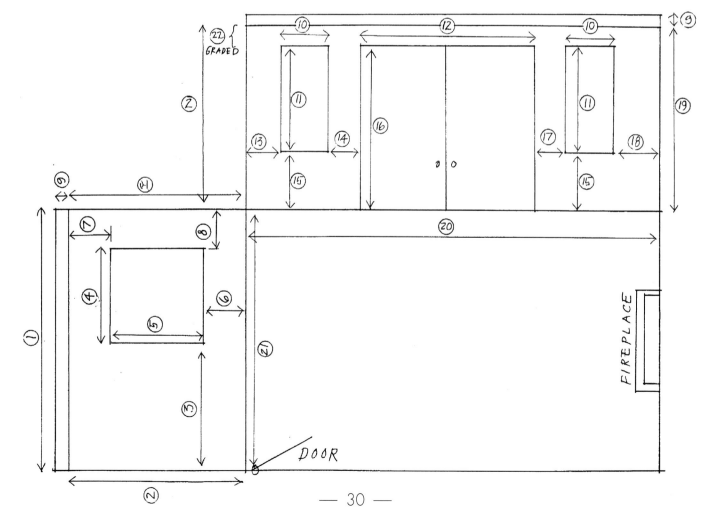

▼ (c) Taking measurements of a window to fit blinds inside or outside the reveal:

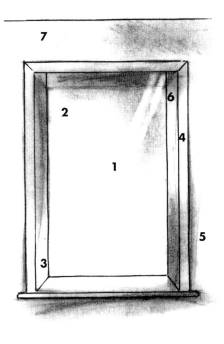

1 Width of the window from side to side of the reveal (check that it is the same top and bottom)
2 Measurement from the soffit to the sill (check that it is the same on both sides)
3 Measurement of the depth of the reveal
4 Width of the architrave
5 Desired finished length of the blind if fitted outside the reveal
6 Desired finished width of the blind if fitted outside the reveal
7 Depth of 'dead light' area between base of cornice and architrave or soffit

▲ White rods with matching rings carry the short curtains and café curtains. The latter are useful when privacy is required and net curtains would not be adequate.

▼ (d) Taking measurements for curtains, pelmets and tiebacks:

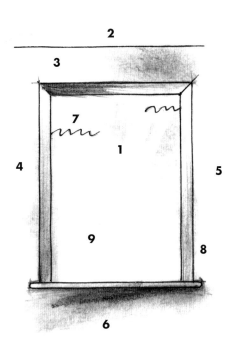

1 Measurement from side to side of the architrave or reveal
2 Measurement for desired length of pelmet board
3 Depth of 'dead light' area between base of cornice and architrave or soffit
4 Length from top of pelmet board to floor, or to desired length for the curtain
5 Length from top of track to floor, or to desired length for the curtain
6 Depth between base of sill and floor
7 Measurement from top of pelmet board to highest point for the pelmet
8 Width of the architrave
9 Estimated length of tieback embrace

▲ Pencil pleat heading tape has been used for this very simple valance.

—— ESTIMATING FOR FABRIC QUANTITIES ——

You will need to know the width of the fabric and the pattern repeat (see page 20).

Rule of thumb: the width of the track is doubled to find out the width of fabric required.

The lengths will be cut to what is called a raw measurement. This is the length from the top of the track (or base of the rings in the case of poles) to the desired length at the level of the windowsill or the floor plus 25–30 cm (10–12 in) for hems and heading turnings. This is a rough calculation:

Length from top of track to floor	2.77 m (109 in)
Heading and hem allowance	30 cm (12 in)
Raw measurement length	3.07 m (121 in)

Allowances must be made for the pattern repeat if the face material has a design on it. The rule of thumb, which works very well, is to allow one pattern repeat per width less one – for four raw measurement lengths you add an allowance of three pattern repeats (see sample calculations on page 33).

You will also need to know, roughly, how much the standard types of curtain headings will draw up.

STANDARD SINGLE POCKET HEADING TAPE

For this type of heading multiply the track length by 2, see fig. 12.

PENCIL PLEAT HEADING TAPE

For this type of heading multiply the track length by 2–2.5, depending on thickness of fabrics, see fig. 13.

Fig. 12

▲ (a) Standard single pocket heading tape.

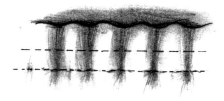

▲ (b) Tape drawn up.

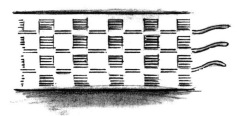

Fig. 13

▲ (a) Pencil pleat heading tape.

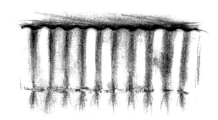

▲ (b) Tape drawn up.

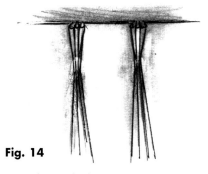

Fig. 14

▲ Triple French pleats.

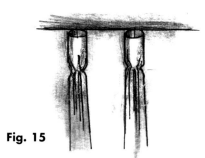

Fig. 15

▲ Goblet pleats.

TRIPLE FRENCH PLEATS AND GOBLET PLEATS

For these types of headings you will be making a mathematical calculation in order to achieve an accurate fabric estimate. On average Triple French Pleats need 15 cm (6 in) of width to each pleat and Goblet Pleats need about 12 cm (4¾ in) of width to each pleat. They are made using (fusible) heading buckram. A simple method for calculating the number of pleats required is outlined in the section on making up handmade headings (page 59). See figs. 14 and 15.

Useful Basic Fabric Estimating Formulae

You will already have taken the measurement of the track from end to end and the finished length or 'drop' which each curtain will require. The length of the drop will depend on the styling and the type of track or pole.

Using Standard One-pocket Tape (1.5–2 x Track Length)

EXAMPLE:

Track length 5.2 m (204¾ in) x 1.5	=	7.8 m	(307⅛ in)
120 cm (47¼ in) wide fabric x 7 widths	=	8.4 m	(330¾ in)
x 6 widths	=	7.2 m	(283½ in)

So estimate on the larger quantity and cut away the excess if necessary. The number of widths required is, therefore, seven.

Drop 3.1 m (122 in) + 25 cm (10 in) turning allowance   =3.35 m (132 in) x 7 = 23.45 m   (923½ in)

Add pattern repeat – e.g. 40 cm (15¾ in) – for 6 drops   =   2.40 m   (94½ in)

Order 26 m (28⅜ yd).   Total =   25.85 m   (1018 in)

Using Pencil Pleat Heading Tape (2–2.5 x Track Length)

EXAMPLE:

Track length 5.2 m (204¾ in) x 2.5	= 13.0 m	(512 in)
120 cm (47¼ in) wide fabric x 11 widths	= 13.2 m	(519¾ in)

The number of widths required is, therefore, 11.

Drop 3.1 m (122 in) + 25 cm (10 in) turning allowance = 3.35 m (132 in) x 11 =   36.85 m (1451 in)
Add pattern repeat – e.g. 40 cm (15¾ in) for 10 drops   =   4.00 m (157½ in)4.00 m (157½ in)

40.85 m (1608½ in)

Order 41 m (44½ yd).

For Triple French and Goblet Pleat Headings

Divide the track length by 10 which will give the number of pleats required. Each pleat will take up 15 cm (6 in) of fabric.

EXAMPLE:

Fabric for pleats	1.50 m	(60 in)
Track length	1.00 m	(39 in)
Ease	.10 m	(4 in)
Turning allowances	.08 m	(3¼ in)
Width required =	2.68 m	(106¼ in)

Divide the width required by the width of the chosen fabric, say, 140 cm (56 in), which will give an excess of 12 cm (4¾ in) – this amount can easily be taken up in the pleats and seams.

FRILLS

Work out, in advance, what width you want the frills to be, remembering to add seam allowances and then work out how many widths you will get from a metre (yard) of fabric. With a patterned fabric you are likely to have pattern repeat offcuts to draw on. Frilling does not have to pattern match at the seams.

You estimate for frilling in the same way as for anything which is gathered: double the length of whatever it is to go on or in. For example, a curtain with a finished length of 2.5 m (98 in) will need 5 m (196 in) of strip to be gathered back to a frill of 2.5 m (98 in). More information on frilling is given on page 97.

CONTRAST-BOUND LEADING EDGE

The fabric estimate must be for the full length of the raw length curtain measurement as there cannot be a join in the fabric on a contrast-bound leading edge. This is very wasteful of material if there is to be only one pair of curtains but not if several pairs of curtains are being made. Contrast binding on frilling may use up some of the excess. Do not use a contrast fabric which is not of the same weight, fibre content and quality as the face fabric because they will 'fight' one another if they are not matched. A narrow band of contrast, such as that shown as Type Two frilling (page 101), will require a strip cut 4 cm (1⅜ in) wide.

FRINGES, ROPES AND BRAIDS

Quantities for fringes, ropes and braids will depend upon how complicated the pattern of their application is to be. A knot in a heavy rope can take as much as 20–40 cm (8–16 in) of rope, so experiment first to find out how much will be needed to achieve the styling required. Ropes, fringes, braids, fan edgings and so on can be very expensive and it is a matter for pride if you finish a job with only 50 cm (20 in) in hand. Do not forget to add turning allowances to the estimate.

◀ Handmade triple French pleats are considered to be an advanced technique, but they are not difficult to achieve and their use makes curtains hang beautifully.

▶ The shaping for these fringed pelmets is virtually the same as for the smocked ones shown on the frontispiece. The goblet pleats are well defined and have been decorated with knotted rope.

WORKING OUT FABRIC ESTIMATES

Before embarking on compiling a fabric estimate, draw up a 'grid'. Make a list of every item which the window or room is to have to jog your memory. Note how much fabric is required for each item separately on the grid. Keep the completed grid after the job is finished because it could prove a useful reference in the future should a disaster happen. The curtains could be damaged in a fire or flood, or could even be stolen.

You will see from the grid that the lining and interlining quantities for fairly straightforward pelmets and valances are the same as the total of the raw length quantities. In order to be economical with the fabrics you will be cutting each width marginally shorter – 5 cm (2 in) or so – but this is a 'perk' to which you are entitled. You should use a different weight of interlining for the curtains from that which you use for the pelmet or valance – this is to save a little weight.

Swags and tails will take much less interlining than they will probably take of fabric fabric, especially if the latter is printed with a large pattern repeat. This is because you can use the interlinings sideways or top-to-bottom and fit your cut shapes on to the interlining in rather the same way that you would arrange the pieces of a dress pattern on a length of dress material (page 119).

Do not forget that tie-backs need to be placed on the face fabric in such a way that, as far as possible, the same pattern motif will appear in the same place on each one. The chosen motif

5, Jan '95

Mrs D.R. Smith – Brecknock House
"Warner" Roses 137W 72 Patt. Rpt.

DRAWING ROOM	RAW LENGTH	FINISHED LENGTH	FACE FABRIC	LINING	INTER-LINING	DOM-ETTE	GREEN CONTRAST	COS[…]
CURTAINS (3 WIDTHS)								
SIDE WINDOW	3·00 118 1/8 in	2·70 106 1/4 in	10·44 411 1/16 in	9·00 354 3/8 in	9·00 354 3/8 in	–	–	X
BAY (7 WIDTHS)	3·00 118 1/8 in	2·65 104 in	22·87 900 3/4 in	21·00 826 7/8 in	21·00 826 7/8 in	–	–	
LARGE SWAGS (X6)	1·44 56 11/16 in	·45 17 3/4 in	8·64 340 3/16 in	6·00 236 1/4 in	–	6·00 236 1/4 in		X
SMALL SWAGS (X2)	1·00 39 3/8 in	·30 11 13/16 in	–	2·00 78 3/4 in	–	2·00 78 3/4 in	2·00 78 3/4 in	–
GREEN BACKING	·50 19 3/4 in	·27 10 5/6 in	–	2·50 98 1/2 in	–	–	2·50 98 1/2 in	X
TAILS (X4)	2·88 113 3/8 in	2·25 88 1/2 in	11·52 455 19/32 in	–	–	7·00 275 5/8 in	7·00 275 5/8 in	X
TIE-BACKS (X6)			OFF CUTS					
TOTALS	–	–	53·47 2105 3/8 in	40·50 1594 3/4 in	30·00 1181 1/4 in	15·00 590 5/8 in	11·50 452 7/8 in	X

Order:– Face Fabric 55m (60 1/4 yds)
Lining 41 m (44 7/8 yds)
Interlining 30 m (32 7/8 yds)
Domette 15 m (16 1/2 yds)
Green contrast 11·50m (12 1/2 yds)

Fig. 16

▶ Sample grid for fabric estimating and making up charges.

may be different for the right-hand side from that chosen for the left-hand side, but all the right-hand sides *must* show the same motif as one another, as must those for the left-hand sides. This can consume a lot of material. Do not forget, either, that tie-backs must be lined on their inner face – offcuts of face fabric can be used if they are big enough, or a contrast colour or ordinary lining material, but consider including your choice in your estimate.

It is wise to round up your fabric estimates and then to add a little to deal with contingencies. By 'a little', I do mean just that – an exaggerated over-estimate, knowingly achieved, is thoroughly dishonest.

Fabric estimates take time and care to work out, so allow plenty of uninterrupted time in which to do it. You will need your workbook, paper and pencils, your expanding tape measure, a calculator and a drink of something soothing when you have finished!

If possible your estimate should be typed on headed A4 writing paper. Make two or three copies – one for yourself, one for the client and one for luck. Make your estimate as detailed as possible and include sketches drawn roughly to scale to illustrate what has been decided. It is better, however, to omit the total of the making-up charges as this would probably be the first thing the client would notice on unfolding the letter before realizing how much work is involved.

THE SOFT FURNISHING WORKROOM

----
17 SOMEPLACE ROAD, ANYTOWN, SP2 7XZ

Mrs I Austin-Jones   February
12 Bendally Road
Collingwood
Surrey

Dear Mrs Austin-Jones

ESTIMATE: Two windows for smaller spare room

Interlined curtains to have single width per side to a track length of 119.5 cm (47 in) and 110.5 cm (43⁵⁄₁₆ in). Drop on left 2.43 m (95¹¹⁄₁₆ in) and 2.45 m (96⁹⁄₃₂ in) on right.

Pelmets to be narrow ruched bands between green contrast piping with simple, gathered 'skirt'. Finished length 23 cm (9 in). Two required – one for each window.

Ruched tie-backs (4) to match ruching of pelmet in style.

		Cost
Making:	4 widths interlined curtains with multi-pocket tape headings	xx
	4 crescent-shaped tie-backs, ruched and piped to match pelmets	xx
	2 pelmets, piped, ruched and skirted with top band on hardboard	xx
	Green contrast	xx
	Brass tie-back hooks x 4 @ x	xx
	Curtain hooks etc. for hanging @ x per window	xx
	Travel	xx
	Hanging time charged at x per hour 3 hours?	

Face fabric required 14 m (15³⁄₈ yd). Lining required 11.50 m (12½ yd). Interlining 11.50 m (12½ yd) Domette 2.5 m (2¾ yds). I can supply lining at xx per metre (yard), mid-weight interlining at xx per metre (yard) and domette at xx per metre (yard).

Should you accept this estimate, I will require an advance of xx to cover the cost of the linings etc.

Yours sincerely

BASIC CURTAIN-MAKING TECHNIQUES

4

Whether you are making unlined, lined or interlined curtains, there are a few basic principles which will help you to achieve a professional finish to your work. They are all easy to follow and will soon become instinctive.

— Cut panels of fabric on the straight, using a T-square to do so

— Interlock linings (on each seam, on each half width and 15cm (6 in) in from the side folds)

— Interlock interlinings (on each seam, at each quarter width and 15 cm (6 in) in from the side folds)

— Weights should be covered with lining material (page 45) and placed at each seam, each half width, and into each corner of the hem

— Have seams lying on top of seams to minimize ugly shadows when the curtain is seen drawn closed against sunlight

— Trim seams to 1.5 cm (⅝ in) this opens out to be 3 cm (1³⁄₁₆ in)

— Cut away tight selvage edges before machining up the seam

— Pattern joining and matching should be as perfect as possible

— Use pure cotton thread for sewing up natural fibre fabrics and thread with a man-made fibre content for man-made fabrics

— Machine the seams from hem to heading

— Mark/identify each drop or part of the curtain with a 'code' so that the right pieces go together

— Use really good quality heading tape

▲ Smocking makes an attractive heading for a pelmet valance and is not diff to do. It is an effective treatment, especially for a bedroom.

UNLINED CURTAINS

Sheer or net curtains come under this category. Unlined curtains are not really to be recommended because they are very thin and without the protection of a lining, they will deteriorate quite quickly. Unlined curtains can be used in cloakrooms, kitchens and bathrooms as they are likely to be washed quite frequently. Washing can shrink curtain fabric by up to 7 per cent and you should point this fact out to your client. It is worth remembering the undoubted uses of detachable linings for unlined curtains which are to be washed often – a special heading tape is available which encloses the top raw edge of the lining material and which is held in place with the same set of hooks used to suspend the curtain.

LINED CURTAINS

Lined-only curtains are the most usual and popular because they cost less than interlined ones. Most ready-made curtains are 'lined-only' and machine-stitching is used for the hems and side turnings. Lined-only curtains are sufficient to insulate double-glazed windows, or for windows in hot climates. Because lined-only curtains look rather thin, you may like to give them a more generous look by adding an extra drop or two if there is sufficient 'stack-back' room.

INTERLINED CURTAINS

These are curtains which are made of a sandwich of three layers of fabric, the middle layer being bump or interlining. Interlined curtains look and feel sumptuous giving a room a sense of luxury and quiet because they absorb noise as well as insulate against draughts. Silk curtains really must be interlined to plump up the thin fabric

and to protect the face material against the ravages of light and air.

VALANCES

For all the above methods of making curtains, the valances should be of similar construction but a lighter weight of interlining can be used to make interlined pelmet valances or swags and tails.

CURTAIN HEADINGS

These fall into two main categories: those using commercial heading tape to draw them up and those using heading buckram to stiffen the top of the curtain before it is drawn up into handmade pleats. The former is the easiest because it is easy to adjust for width. The latter creates a far superior curtain, but the width is not adjustable.

CHECK THE FABRIC

It is worth checking the fabric for faults in the colour and pattern as soon as it is delivered because if there are any, it should be returned to the sender immediately. You should check at least 10 m (11 yd) of each bolt for faults before starting to cut. The bolts will always be delivered with a notice warning you to check the material for quantity and faults before cutting as the supplier will not give a refund on fabric which has already been cut – these notices are the supplier's legal 'get out'. Check the delivery note to ensure that the right amount has been sent – this is especially important with hand-blocked prints, which are not only expensive but also may no longer be available should there be a discrepancy between what was ordered and what was supplied.

Mark the delivery note with the client's name and what it is to be used for – for example, Mrs. Brown, red

contrast for No. 1 bedroom curtains. Keep the delivery notes for some months after you have finished the job. Interior decorators often like to have these notes sent to them eventually for their own records.

Faults that you are likely to find include offset printing, blurred colours, uneven colour intensity, holes and tears, water stains, overprinted creases, straight lines which are crooked, lines of thicker weft or warp thread, and pattern drift.

It is particularly necessary to look for faults if the client tells you that he or she has found a fabric at a bargain price – there is usually something wrong with it! You will soon reach the point where you will not be interested in making up cheap fabrics or seconds.

PATTERN DRIFT

It is particularly important to check for pattern drift. This can be done in two ways: by testing the straightness of the printing against a T-square or by turning the material so that the wrong side faces you and then bringing the selvage edges into the middle – if the pattern does not join, the fabric either has pattern drift or a half-drop repeat.

Manufacturers feel that a drift of up to 2.5 cm (1 in) is reasonable so you will have to decide whether or not the pattern drift is acceptable to you. If not, discuss the problem with your client and try to return the material to the manufacturer and get another batch delivered.

Re-rolling the bolt is slightly easier if you roll it towards you across the width of the table rather than down its length.

A slight pattern drift – up to 2 cm (¾ in) – can be dealt with quite easily unless you are making curtains for a large picture, bow or bay window. With many drops of fabric in a continuous sweep, the pattern drift will build up from 2 cm (¾ in) on one outside edge to multiples of that amount over on the other outside edges and this will give the curtains a lop-sided look. On curtains which are for separate windows, even if they are on the same wall, the drift can be disguised by having the same motif as the starting point on all the same outside

edges so that the effect of the drift is staggered. See Fig. 17.

It is also possible to have a combination of half-drop repeat and pattern drift and this is very difficult to detect in advance. It is always best to cut the first raw length and then to pattern match each following width before cutting and coding (pages 40–41).

Remember that a pattern drift is similar to a half-drop repeat and if you are going to have to split one of the lengths down the middle, make sure that it will match the full lengths to which it is to be joined. Do this by cutting the length to be split over-long (see the section dealing with cutting and joining half-drop repeats, pages 40–41).

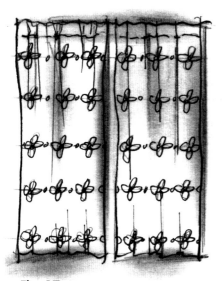 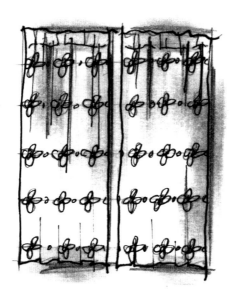 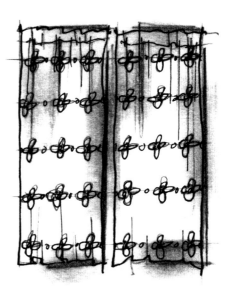

Fig. 17

▲ Making the starting point for each set of curtains at each window the same helps to break up the ascending lines of pattern drift, so it is less obvious.

CUTTING FABRICS

Face fabrics usually come off the bolt with the right side to the inside (to help to prevent dirtying and damage). Lining fabrics usually come off the bolt right side out.

Take a good look at the fabric and 'get to know' it. You may never have seen it before or, at best, seen only a small sample. Have the material facing you right side up and fold the cut end under here and there to decide which part of the pattern looks best at the hemline. This decision depends

entirely upon the pattern and your taste but try not to kill off a bird or a flower by cutting through their middle! The pattern should be kept level right round the room for all the items you are making – for instance, if you are going to make a Roman blind for one of the windows, the pattern placement should match the pattern placement of the curtains.

This requires some careful calculations which you should have taken into consideration when

measuring up with the hem of the Roman blind calculated to be such and such a distance from the floor.

When you have chosen the hemline, put a pin, sideways, into the selvage to mark the point. Now measure up the selvage to find the finished length and mark this point with a sideways pin too. Add the correct hem allowance for the type of hem you are making – 6 cm (2⅜ in) for an interlined curtain and 12 cm (4¾ in) for a lined-only curtain – and mark the point with a pin. Above the pin inserted to mark the top measurement add 10–15 cm (4–6 in). Once cut, in a completely straight line, at the top and the bottom pin, the result will be a length of fabric giving the raw measurement or raw length which will be the 'template' for cutting all the other lengths. For cutting fabric with a pattern drift, see page 39.

Choose one side or the other of the raw length as the leading edge of the curtain. The term 'leading edge' means the folded edges of the curtains that draw together at the middle of the window. If the room has several windows, start with the window on the left of the door and work towards the window on the right of the door. The choice for the leading edge may be self-evident if, for instance, the material has a patterned border. Identify each length of fabric by pencilling a code on the selvage and at the top so that you will know exactly where it is going to be used – for example, No. 1 W – LE – LHS – FL 2.8 m (110¼ in), meaning No. 1 Window – Leading Edge – Left-hand Side – Finished Length 2.8 m (110¼ in). See Fig. 18.

When cutting plain fabrics it is essential to mark the material as you proceed so that you maintain the same face and direction of weave when you come to sewing it up. Mark the top of each length of material with a cut notch and the wrong side with easily visible chalked lines. On plain satin weaves and velvets, for instance, the weave or nap catches the light in different ways depending on which way up the fabric is used and you would not want to have 'up' on one width and 'down' on another as this would give the curtains a strange, 'striped' look.

Allow the cut lengths to 'relax' for at least 24 hours after cutting because the material has often been tightly wound on to the bolt for months and it will shrink very, very slightly once it is unrolled and cut.

On anything other than a half-drop repeat cutting is, really, quite easy. Just use the raw measurement length of fabric as the guide and, coding as you go along, cut the second width to match the pattern of the first, the third to match the second and so on. If you use bulldog clips to suspend the lengths, one on top of the next, at the side of the table,

you can see exactly what you are doing.

With a half-drop repeat you need to be careful about cutting those lengths which are to be cut in half down the middle, see Fig. 19. These split widths must be cut over-long by the full pattern repeat to ensure that the half-drop can be moved into the correct position on one of the half sides. If you get this wrong, the result will be as

Fig. 18

▷ Coded lengths.

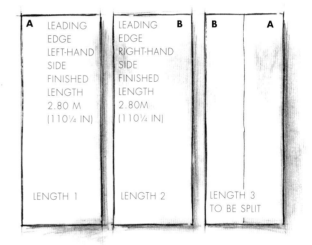

Fig. 19

▽ Half-drop repeat – cut length 3 over-long by a full pattern repeat to ensure that the split width will pattern-match on the left-hand side.

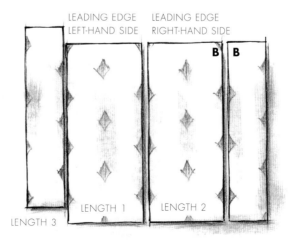

shown in Fig. 19 and it is an expensive business to replace fabric which has been wrongly cut like this!

LINING AND INTERLINING

Lining and interlining should be cut 10 cm (4 in) shorter than the face fabric raw length measurements. These bolts and rolls are very big and difficult to handle. It is helpful to unroll a good deal of lining and push it all back to the end of the table, pulling the lengths towards you and cutting them off until you need to unroll some more. Interlining often comes fan-folded in widths of approximately 1 m (yd). Heaving the whole bolt up on to the table can take real strength but it is relatively easy to pull the lengths off and to measure them with the cutting kept straight by using a weft thread as a cutting guide.

Fold all the lengths across their width and in such a way that you can see the code easily and keeping everything for each window separate from that for the next window. Pin a sheet of paper to the top of the pile and note which window it is intended for.

Lining is frequently folded in half on the bolt and these lengths of material should be left lying on top of one another to the required number for the job being done, before being folded for temporary storage. A pair of curtains requiring three widths of face fabric will also need three widths of lining fabric, so take three cut lengths of lining fabric and without opening out the manufacturer's crease, fold all three layers together at the same time ready for temporary storage. The reason for this is explained on the next page.

▷ The stark drama of the wide blue and white stripes is softened by the patterned lining. Make sure that the outline of any patterned lining cannot be seen when the curtains are illuminated by sunlight.

JOINING FABRICS

To avoid wasting time when joining fabrics, it is essential to work on an assembly line basis. This requires some advance preparation.

Start by making sure that the sewing machine is well oiled (and cleaned so that no oil spots get onto the fabrics) and that a new, fine (size 12) needle is in place. Check the stitch tension on a scrap of the fabric and adjust it if it is not perfect. Use a stitch length which will give you 8–10 stitches to 2.5 cm (1 in) – it is not necessary to have a short stitch length for the making of most curtains.

If the machine does not have an automatic bobbin winding facility, load a number of bobbins with sewing thread. A bobbin can hold roughly 18 m (19½ yd) of thread.

Cut out several strips, all about 30 cm (12 in) long but of different widths (see Fig. 20), in lightweight card for measuring hems and side turnings. Using these strips will not only save time but also give your work accuracy and a professional finish.

JOINING LINING

Join the lengths of lining first. The seam allowance should be 2 cm (¾ in) but if the selvage is particularly tight, you may have to allow a little more. Without separating the layers of the component lengths, cut along the manufacturer's crease for any lengths which need splitting in half. 'Fan fold' them so that the hem edge is uppermost. Lift all the fan-folded layers together and take them to the machine, settle the fabric on your lap and, using Fig. 21 as a guide, machine the lengths together right side to right side. The joy of this method is that the right side is automatically to the right side. Once all the seams have been joined, turn all the fabric so that you

get easy access to the hem edge and, with your fingers, fold in a 1 cm (⅜ in) turning allowance followed by a 5 cm (2 in) turning to make the hem. This job is accurate and easy if you use a 15 cm (6 in) metal measuring gauge, or the 5 cm (2 in) wide strip of card. Machine the hem up as close to the edge of the fold-back as possible – make sure that the vertical seams are

opened out and flat before machining over them. Refold these joined lengths carefully to cause the least amount of creasing, and return them to the right pile of fabrics for storage until they are used.

Continue with the joining and hemming of the lining until this part of the work has been done for the entire job because changing sewing machine

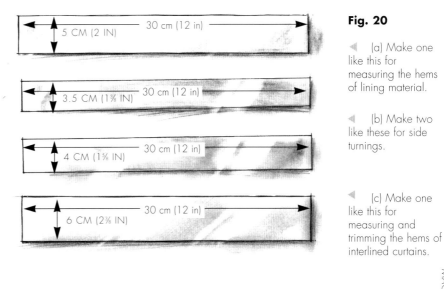

Fig. 20

◁ (a) Make one like this for measuring the hems of lining material.

◁ (b) Make two like these for side turnings.

◁ (c) Make one like this for measuring and trimming the hems of interlined curtains.

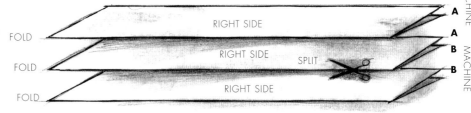

Fig. 21

▲ (a) Keep the folded layers of lining together so that right side can be machined to right side automatically – A to A, B to B and so on – and the hemming completed across all the widths before the half widths are cut.

▷ (b) 'Fan fold' the layers of lining for presentation to the machine, folding back those which are not being worked upon.

feet and altering the flow of work interrupts your thought progression and wastes time.

There is usually enough dressing in lining material to enable you to finger press seams open. Actual pressing, with an iron, can be left until the curtains are completely made up.

JOINING INTERLINING

The problem with joining interlining is that the fabric is so soft, fluffy and (usually) loosely woven that one layer of material creeps and travels over the other as it is being fed through the machine. Without prior tacking or pinning this causes the lengths to finish up uneven and 'stepped' at either the heading or the hem. Tacking is, however time-consuming and difficult (the fluff adheres to the tacking thread causing lumps and knots) and pins fall out. A solution to this difficulty is to use a large number of bulldog clips instead. Lay two lengths of the interlining together on the table, bring the hem edges to the level, the selvages to be on line and with one another and both the layers to feel comfortable and unforced; then clip the selvages together with the bulldog clips placed at intervals of about 20 cm (8 in).

Set the sewing machine up to do the largest zigzag stitch of which it is capable and then open out the two layers of interlining on the table so that they look like a book with the bulldog clips uppermost. Push the top towards the hem level down the length of the table and then carefully lift and carry the material to the machine sitting so that the bulldog clips are resting in your lap and the material will present to the machine hemline first. Remove the first clip and bring the selvage of one layer of the material over to cover the one underneath by about 1 cm (⅜ in). Make sure that the

thread has a good long tail and that the needle is inserted into the fabric before starting to machine (doing this helps to prevent cobbling.)

Zigzag the two layers together as neatly as possible (see Fig. 22), keeping the 1 cm (⅜ in) allowance as even as possible and removing the clips as they come up. If there is a problem of one layer of the interlining travelling and building up into a possible pucker or fold before the next clip, stop the machine and ease the excess fabric back towards the needle before continuing with the zigzagging towards the next clip. Return to the table to clip the next length of interlining in place and continue the process until all the lengths are made up into the required component parts. Fold for temporary storage and return to the correct pile.

PREPARING THE FACE FABRIC FOR JOINING AND MACHINING

Take two of your 'coded' lengths and make sure that they are compatible. Fling one of these lengths on to the table, right side up and with the selvage to be joined facing you. It is probably most convenient if the top of the pattern is to your right. Smooth this length flat with a wooden yardstick.

Place the second length on top of the first right side down and with the pattern facing in the same direction. Get the two selvage edges to be on line

with one another, moving the pattern upwards or downwards until, when you roll the two layers of face fabric apart just slightly, you can see whether or not the patterns are going to join accurately. Choose a nice, easy-to-find strong motif as the anchoring point and finger-fold or iron the top layer back to make a crease which lines up exactly with the two sides of the pattern to be joined. Pin the two layers of material together so that the pins are put in with their points facing towards you but far back enough from the creased line to be well out of the way of the machine stitching. See Fig. 23. Putting the pins in this way will enable you to machine the layers together without continually stopping and starting and you will, therefore, achieve a straighter seam line. Flip the fold forward, clear of the pin points, and machine carefully down the creased line. The bulk of the material should, of course, be to the left of the machine needle.

Do not attempt to machine patterned fabric together without first pinning. The layers can travel and the pattern can become badly misaligned. Once the machine stitching has been done, trim the seams back to a width of 1.5 cm (⅝ in) and snip them on the diagonal at 15 cm (6 in) intervals if necessary.

Fig. 22
▲ Use the longest, widest zigzag stitch to join interlining. Overlap the edges by about 1 cm (⅜ in).

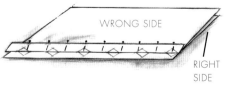

Fig. 23
▲ Using the described method, joining face fabric is easy, quick and efficient.

COVERING WEIGHTS

All curtains need to have weights placed in the fold of the hem. The weights should be covered with lining fabric. Having the weights sewn into a little bag makes them very much easier to sew and hold in place within the fold of the hem. There are a number of ways to make the bags but the easiest method is to make a long tube just a little wider than the width of the

weight. Slip the weight into the open end of the tube and sew across the tube above and below the weight at the same time as the weight is sewn into the hemline. See Fig. 24.

Weights should be placed in the corners of the hem of a curtain and at every half width on lined-only curtains, and at every width on interlined curtains.

Fig. 24

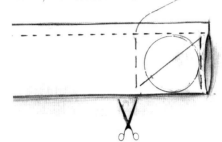

Make a tube from lining and insert the weights. Sew into place as they are needed.

STITCHES USED IN CURTAIN-MAKING

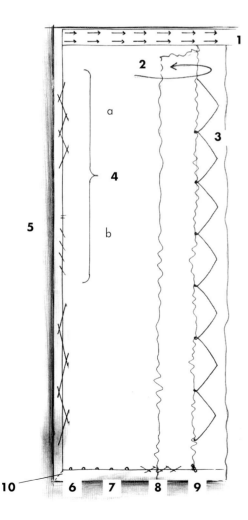

Fig. 25

Stitches used in curtain-making

1 Long machine stitch – to attach the heading tape. Both lines of stitching must travel in the same direction or the heading tape will distort. Use thread which matches the face fabric.

2 Interlining folded back.

3 Lock stitch – a lengthy version of blanket stitch which picks up one or two threads from the wrong side of the face fabric with very loose stitches placed roughly 15–20 cm (6–8 in) – a hand span apart – down the length of each width at each seam line, each quarter width and 15 cm (6 in) from the side turnings. Start or end this stitching about 15 cm (6 in) down from the finished top length and start or finish about 10 cm (4 in) above the hemline.

4 Side turnings are stitched down with herring-bone stitch (a) or with serge stitch (b). Use a very open version of herringbone stitch to hold down the side turns of lined-only curtains, catching only one or two threads of the face fabric.

5 Machine-stitching – used for joining the lengths and putting up the hems of linings. Stitch length should be 8 –10 to 2 cm (¾ in).

6 Slip-stitch – used to attach the lining to the curtain down the sides.

7 Slip/blind hemming – for the hemline of lined-only curtains.

8 Herring-bone stitch for the hem of interlined curtains.

9 'Virginia Twist' – to make a bridge between the hem of the face fabric and the hem of the lining.

10 'Ladder stitch' – to join the folds of the mitre.

Fig. 26

▼ (a) Lock stitch should be about this size. Make the stitches loose enough to create an imaginary square. The starting and finishing knots should be *on* the interlining. The starting and finishing knots should be *on* the lining of lined-only curtains.

▲ (b) Herring-bone stitch for the hems of interlined curtains should be about this size. But herring-bone stitch used to catch back the side turnings of lined-only curtains can have 10 cm (4 in) between the insertion point of each stitch.

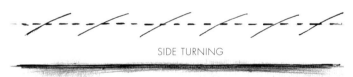

▲ (c) Slip-stitching of the lining to the side turnings should be about this size. Do not pull the stitches up too tight if using this stitch to sew a double-folded hem.

SIDE TURNING

▲ (d) Serge stitch for the side turnings should be about this size.

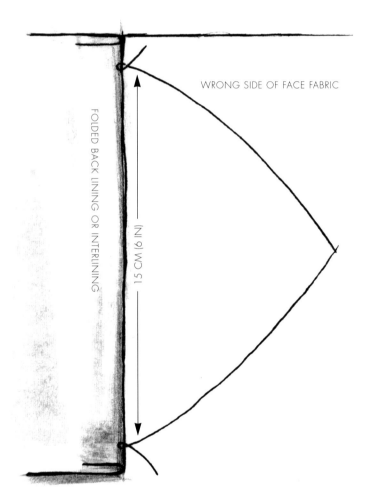

WRONG SIDE OF FACE FABRIC

FOLDED BACK LINING OR INTERLINING

15 CM (6 IN)

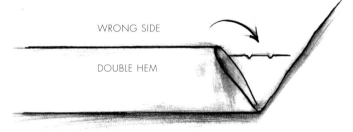

WRONG SIDE

DOUBLE HEM

▲ (e) Blind hemming for lined-only curtains is stitched below the top fold of the hem between the wrong side of the face fabric and the folded hem.

TIP
Protectors for the fingers you use when hand-sewing can be made from old rubber gloves. Choose fingertips which fit snugly and cut them just a little bit shorter than the first knuckle of the relevant finger.

MITRING CORNERS

It is not necessary to cut fabric away to create a mitre. Indeed, in curtains it is foolish to do so because it would obviate the possibility of lengthening in the future.

Learn to do mitres really well. They should look almost as if the folds have been machine-stitched together, and there should be no 'mouse's ear' at the outer corner. This is the part of a curtain which is most often examined to judge the quality of your work.

Depending upon whether you are making a lined-only curtain or an interlined curtain, there are slight variations to the method of constructing a mitre and inserting the weights (pages 50 and 54).

Fig. 27

▷ (a) Fold the hem upwards by 6 cm (2⅜ in). Fold the side turning in by 4 cm (1⅝ in). Press the resulting corner gently to make creased guidelines when the material is unfolded. Put a pin right in the lowest corner of the *inside* of the sharp angle of the fold – pin into the actual table top if the surface is suitable, otherwise use an old magazine.

◁ (b) Keeping the pin in place, open up the side edge and then the hem to create a diagonal fold. Bring the two diagonal edges on either side of the pin together at an angle to the pin. A thin knitting needle helps to lift and move the fabric.

▷ (c) Ladder stitch the mitre together to make a neat join. The stitches should be very small and firmly pulled up. Start at point 'A' with a couple of firm holding stitches and work downwards to the corner. Knot off by inserting the needle back up the inside of one of the angled folds and knot on to one of the stitches at a point which will be hidden by the lining. Take the tail of the knot well back into the fabric before pulling it through and cutting off carefully.

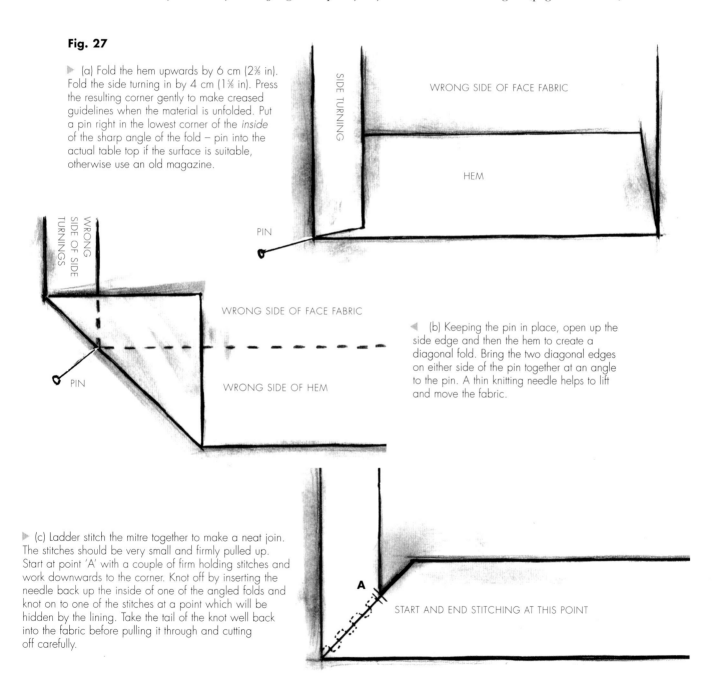

FRENCH SEAMS

It is sometimes necessary to make French seams, for example, when joining fabric lengths of net or sheer fabrics.

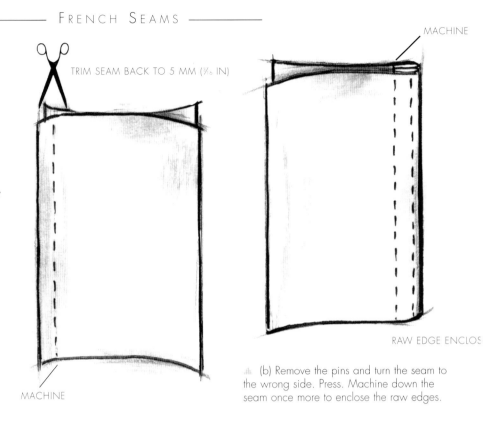

TRIM SEAM BACK TO 5 MM (³⁄₁₆ IN)

MACHINE

RAW EDGE ENCLOS

MACHINE

Fig. 28

▷ (a) Cut away the selvage edges. Pin the raw edges together with the pins put in sideways and away from the machining line (to avoid stopping and starting to take pins out while machining). Machine at the 5 mm (³⁄₁₆ in) mark.

▷ (b) Remove the pins and turn the seam to the wrong side. Press. Machine down the seam once more to enclose the raw edges.

VIRGINIA TWIST

Virginia Twist is basically finger crocheting and was shown to me by one of my students, called Virginia. Use as a 'bridge' between the inside hems of face fabric and lining.

Sew the interlocking as usual from heading to hem on the lining. When you have done the last stitch – about 10 cm (4 in) up from the hem of the curtain – take the free end of the length of thread and make a good, big knot in it. This will double the thread and so make it stronger for the making of the Virginia Twist. Now slip the needle between the hem and the wrong side of the face fabric bringing it out about 1.5 cm (⅝ in) below the top of the hem.

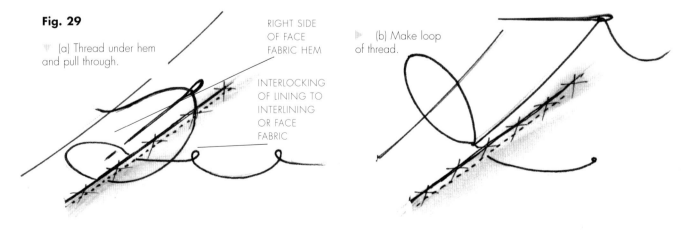

Fig. 29

▽ (a) Thread under hem and pull through.

RIGHT SIDE OF FACE FABRIC HEM

INTERLOCKING OF LINING TO INTERLINING OR FACE FABRIC

▷ (b) Make loop of thread.

Fig. 29 (continued)

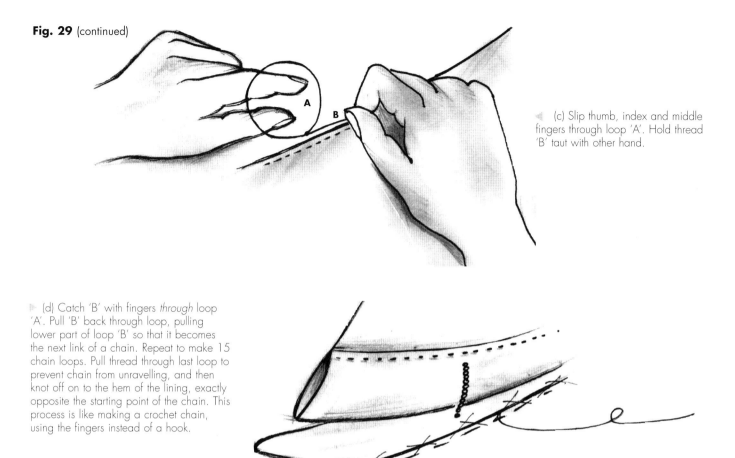

◁ (c) Slip thumb, index and middle fingers through loop 'A'. Hold thread 'B' taut with other hand.

▷ (d) Catch 'B' with fingers *through* loop 'A'. Pull 'B' back through loop, pulling lower part of loop 'B' so that it becomes the next link of a chain. Repeat to make 15 chain loops. Pull thread through last loop to prevent chain from unravelling, and then knot off on to the hem of the lining, exactly opposite the starting point of the chain. This process is like making a crochet chain, using the fingers instead of a hook.

MAKING UP OF SEVERAL LAYERS AND WIDTHS OF FABRICS

Making curtains, with all the necessary processes, is not difficult for a capable needleworker, but what is difficult is handling the huge areas of material to keep the layers under control. As you gain experience, you will tackle the processes of making things up in different ways depending upon the size and styling.

In making large curtains you may have to construct the whole of one side of a curtain (apart from putting on the heading tape) before moving on to the next section.

This involves dealing with the interlocking of the interlining, the stitching of the side turnings, the installation of the weights, the mitring of the corners, the putting up of the hems and the application of the lining on that part of the curtain which is on the table, stitching the hem to as far as you can go and leaving the thread hanging free for further use later on.

When the section on the table is complete (including the measuring off, folding and pinning for the finished length), fold the finished section over to the size of a quarter width, towards the unmade part of the curtain and then pull it back to lie parallel with the left-hand edge of the table. Then lift, a layer at a time, all the unworked layers so that they, too, can be brought forward and worked on section by section making sure constantly that the seams are lying straight down the length of the table, and that you carefully interlock seam to seam.

Although it is difficult, you will probably find yourself able to manage as many as six widths of fabric. More widths than this become too heavy and unwieldy for anyone to handle without help and you will learn, depending on your own size and the size of your workroom, the maximum dimensions you can handle.

MAKING AND LINING CURTAINS

5

When making and lining curtains, a solid familiarity with the basic techniques as described in Chapter 4 will help you to achieve professional results and finishes far more easily.

—————— LINED-ONLY CURTAINS – HAND-STITCHED SIDES AND HEMS ——————

The face fabric for lined-only curtains is constructed to have a double hem. This means that you must have a hem allowance of 12 cm (4¾ in) which will be folded up to 6 cm (2⅜ in) plus 6 cm (2⅜ in). This type of hem looks more attractive, seen against sunlight, than the more usual 1 cm (⅜ in) plus 6 cm (2⅜ in) fold.

Measure off and cut the required number of lengths of face fabric. Split lengthwise those lengths which require halving. Remember to 'code' the lengths at the top (see page 41).

Measure off and cut the required number of widths of lining. The length will be the same as the raw length measurement of the face fabric less 10 cm (4 in) (for the sake of economy). Split lengthwise those widths which require halving, following the instructions on page 42 for the cutting and joining of lining material. Remember to notch the tops of the cut lengths of lining.

Check that the eventual seams for both the face fabric and the lining will lie on top of one another by 'testing' a couple of lengths for their sewn-up width by pinning a few centimetres (inches) of the seam allowances to find out how the two layers will fall together. It is very important that the seams of

the face fabric are on line with the seams of the lining material because lined-only curtains are fairly translucent when seen against sunlight and unaligned seams look untidy and unprofessional. You may have to adjust the lining to get the seams right. Remember that the width of the face fabric and the width of the lining should be the same.

Check the stitch length – 8–10 stitches to 2 cm (¾ in) – and tension on the sewing machine and adjust them if necessary. Machine all the lengths of the materials into their component sections, using the methods described on pages 43–44 for the hems of the linings.

Iron all the seams open, and iron the hems of the lining. Fold and store all those parts upon which you will not immediately be working. Do remember, though, to let the fabrics 'relax' if necessary.

Lay the joined sections of face fabric for one curtain on the table wrong side up. If you are making up a curtain with many widths of material, lay the hem edge to the long side of your work table because the next step will be to put weights in the hem and then to turn it up.

Using a 6 cm (2⅜ in) measuring

card (page 18), fold up and iron 6 cm (2⅜ in) of hem. Fold up the second layer of the double-fold hem by the same amount and iron it too.

Insert a weight in the prepared tube (page 45). Unfold the ironed-up hem with the raw edge of the right side of the fabric facing you. Attach the weight with the fold of the tube on line with the raw edge so that the weight can drop right down into the hem, see Fig. 30 (a) page 52. A covered weight is needed on the very edge of each corner, at each half width and on each seam.

Fold the hem back up and prepare to make the mitres, following the method on page 47, except that this hem is a double one to which the weights have already been attached. Just pretend that there is no weight and that you are dealing with a single 6 cm (2⅜ in) wide layer of hem. Slip-stitch the double folded hem. Practise

▶ As this type of styling is very easy to do, it is a good choice for anyone just starting to make soft furnishings.

on a scrap of fabric, if you are not too confident about tackling this. Mitre the corners according to the instructions on page 47. You will find that the weight tucks into the corner very neatly and that the doubled part of the hem is not too bulky. See Figs. 30 (b), (c), (d) and (e).

Slip-stitch the double folded hem. Make the starting point fairly loose and do not take the stitching down the angle of the mitre. Knot on and knot off on the fold of the hem and not on the wrong side of the face fabric itself. Make sure that all the stitches are evenly spaced and not tightly pulled up to prevent dimpling of the face fabric. See Figs. 30 (f) and (g).

If necessary turn the fabric to have the sides of the curtain aligned with the sides of the table. Stitch down the 4 cm (1⅝ in) side turnings of the curtain, using a really big herring-bone stitch and catching only one or two threads on the wrong side of the face fabric.

With the wrong side of the face fabric uppermost, align the side turnings of one side of the curtain with the side of the table and align

Fig. 30

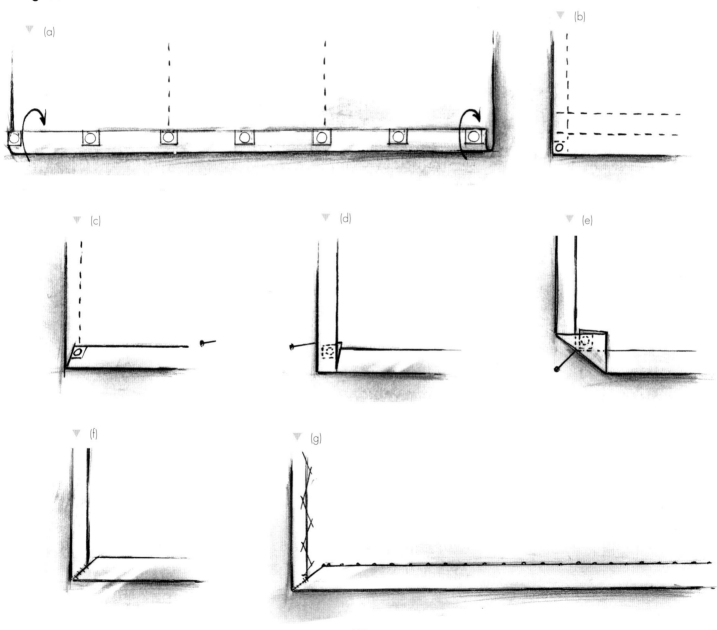

the hem along the end of the table. Keep the fabric in place with bulldog clips. Smooth it all out thoroughly.

Place the already hemmed lining right side up on the face fabric. Seams should lie on top of seams and the hem of the lining should be placed to lie 2 cm (¾ in) above the hem of the face fabric. At the side turnings the lining will probably be over-wide but this does not matter at this stage.

The lining must now be interlocked in place. Fold the lining back until the first seam appears and then interlock the lining seam to the face fabric seam, working from top to hem so that you can finish off with a Virginia Twist (page 48). Bring the lining back towards the side edge and refold it to the half way mark of its width so that you can interlock once again. It is wise to put a further line of interlocking about 15 cm (6 in) in from the side turnings.

The sides of the lining must now be cut down their length to make them fit the curtain. To do this, fold the lining on line with the side edge of the curtain, finger-press the fold and use

the crease as a guide to cutting off the excess lining material.

Now fold the lining back under by 2 cm (¾ in), finger-press and slip-stitch it into place. Make sure that the outer corner of the lining is on line with the angle of the mitre, and that there are 2 cm (¾ in) of face fabric showing at the side turnings and at the hem.

Using a flexible steel rule, measure off the curtain from the hem to the heading to achieve the finished length measurement; make the marks about every 20 cm (8 in) with a soft lead pencil. Use a yardstick to draw a straight line across these marks and then fold both layers of fabric forward, using the pencil line as a guide. See Fig. 31. Trim if necessary.

Prepare the chosen heading tape for use in the next stage. This is where a plastic storage box comes into its own because the big reel of tape, when put into the box, will not roll around and will be easier to handle when you pull the required length straight from the reel – doing this is more economical of tape (except for cartridge pleat heading tape, which must be pinned in

place in advance). With the right side of the tape facing, pull back and out about 10 cm (4 in) of the strings so that they are hanging free. Tie the strands together so that they form a very good knot which cannot become untied. Cut off the de-strung tape to within 3–4 cm (1³⁄₁₆–1⅝ in) of the knot. Change the colour of the sewing thread if necessary.

Take the pinned and folded top edge/heading of the curtain, while it is on the table, and push it away from you so that the top becomes concertinaed. Do the same down the length of the curtain so that it is concertinaed from top to bottom down its length. This enables you to carry the curtain to the machine and to present it in a form whereby the bulk is easier to lift and control. With really large curtains this dodge is vital.

Settle yourself at the machine, with the curtain resting in your lap with the bulk of it to your left, and take the already knotted end of tape (which should feed in from your right) and fold back the raw, de-strung end so that the knot is hidden.

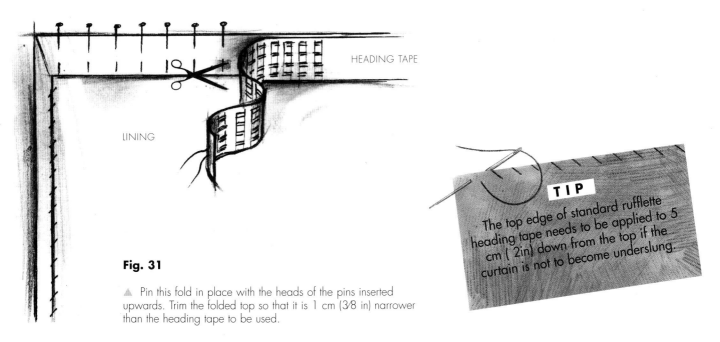

LINING

HEADING TAPE

Fig. 31

▲ Pin this fold in place with the heads of the pins inserted upwards. Trim the folded top so that it is 1 cm (3⁄8 in) narrower than the heading tape to be used.

TIP
The top edge of standard rufflette heading tape needs to be applied to 5 cm (2in) down from the top if the curtain is not to become underslung.

Apply the heading tape so that its top is on line with the top fold of the curtain. You can choose whether to take the tape right to the side fold of the curtain or inset it to be on line with the edge of the lining. In both cases, the raw edge of the top fold of the curtain will have to be tucked up under the fold to conceal it.

Start the stitching of the tape with a few stitches in reverse, if the fabrics are thin enough to allow you to do this without breaking the needle, and then continue right to the other end of the heading as steadily as you can, removing the pins as you go along. But before you quite reach the other end, cut the tape leaving sufficient for you to knot off the strings in the same way as you did at the beginning. Fold the end of the tape under and take the stitching right to the fold. Turn and sew down the folded edge of the tape, finishing with a few reverse stitches. Repeat this process on the lower edge of the tape. The stitching of heading tape must travel in the same direction to allow the pull-up to align correctly.

The curtain is now finished, see Fig. 32. It will only require ironing or pressing and folding (page 58).

HANDMADE INTERLINED CURTAINS

Interlining curtains is more expensive for your clients from the point of view of materials and tailoring, but the cost is outweighed by the advantages of this type of curtain. Choose an interlining which feels 'right' with the face fabric, the type of window and the styling being used, and remember to check that the colours of both the lining and the interlining will not change the colour of the face fabric when seen against daylight.

Interlining curtains will make them last, with proper care, for years longer than lined-only curtains. They hang

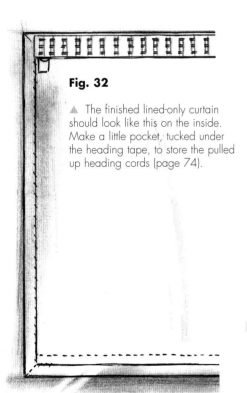

Fig. 32

▲ The finished lined-only curtain should look like this on the inside. Make a little pocket, tucked under the heading tape, to store the pulled up heading cords (page 74).

▷ The rustic appearance of the shepherd's hook pole is echoed by the country-style materials used for the curtains, their linings and the blinds. The pelmet tops are made separately and then headed with the curtains.

much better, look luxurious and feel good. Even relatively cheap face fabric is enhanced by interlining.

If the chosen face fabric is silk, it really must be interlined to help to protect it from atmospheric hazards. Silk curtains look lovely but their life is shortened, by many years, if the windows do not, also, have blinds installed to protect the fabric from the damaging effects of sunlight. If you are asked to make up silk, always try to persuade the client to have simple, translucent roller blinds installed.

MAKING UP INTERLINED CURTAINS

Cut the main fabric, lining and interlining lengths in the same way as already described but allow only 6 cm (2⅜ in) for the hem allowance. Both the lining and the interlining can be cut 10 cm (4 in) shorter than the raw length measurement for the face fabric, to save material.

Join all the lengths of fabrics, using the methods described on pages 43–44.

Lay the face fabric wrong side up on the table, securing one side and the hem edge to the edge of the table with bulldog clips, see Fig. 33 (a). With large curtains it may be that several widths are hanging down on to the floor so you will have to tread carefully!

Lay the interlining on top of the face fabric so that its seams are, as far as possible, lying on top of the seams of the face fabric. Smooth it with a yardstick and your hands to ensure that it is really flat with no air-pockets underneath and that the weave lies straight in both directions. This is important because if the weave of the interlining is askew, the resulting curtains will not hang well. Do not lift and drop the interlining as if it were a table cloth while you are straightening it up – it responds badly to this and the

straightening process difficult. It is much better to move and smooth it gently.

Secure both layers of material with bulldog clips down the edge of the table where the fabrics are falling towards the floor, see Fig. 33 (b). Fold the raw edge of the interlining in half back towards the seam, so that the raw edge is on line with the zigzag seam. Repeat this, taking the fold back to the seam. This gives you the necessary quarter widths to mark the positioning for the interlocking.

Use mercerized thread, in a colour to match the background of the face fabric, to do the interlocking. You will need a length of thread two and a half times the length of the curtain. Controlling such a length is difficult as it picks up fluff from the interlining easily, which causes problems with pulling through and knotting.

Remember the tip about thread on page 15 because it really does come into its own here! Drawing the thread across a block of beeswax also helps.

Work the interlocking from the top

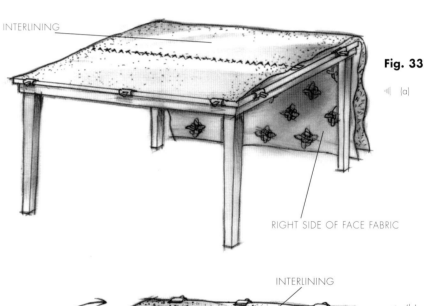

INTERLINING

Fig. 33

◀ (a)

RIGHT SIDE OF FACE FABRIC

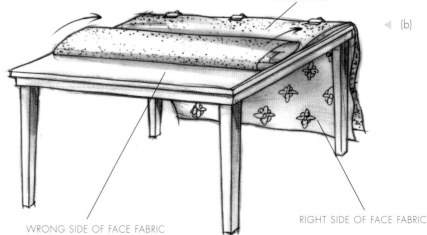

INTERLINING

◀ (b)

WRONG SIDE OF FACE FABRIC

RIGHT SIDE OF FACE FABRIC

to the bottom of the curtain, making sure that you start and finish the stitching about 15 cm (6 in) within the finished length. Knot-on and knot-off to the interlining, making sure that you have a loose stitch to the face fabric.

The stitches for interlocking are large and loose so that when the layers of materials are pulled apart slightly, a sort of loop/bridge appears between the two layers. This is correct. It allows for a slight amount of 'travel' between the layers which is necessary if 'dimpling' is not to be visible on the face fabric when the curtains are hung. There is, of course, movement between all the layers of fabric from their response to atmospheric changes as well as from the effects of handling.

You cannot avoid the task of interlocking interlined curtains because, without it, air will get between the layers and the curtains will balloon to an ever greater extent. They will look fine when first hung, but will gradually take in air and look terrible.

Each line of interlocking must be worked down the quarter widths, folding the interlining back into the necessary position as you go. It is wise, also, to have a line of interlock stitches

15 cm (6 in) away from the coming fold of the side turnings. This line of interlocking helps to hold all the layers firmly at a section of the curtain which gets the hardest wear. It is helpful if this last line of interlocking has a shorter distance between the stitches than those used for the rest of the interlocking.

With the interlocking completed on this first, tabled section of the curtain, there are now three processes to carry out. First sew the weights into place on the interlining. At the seam lines the position for the weight will be on (or just to one side if very bulky) the seam with the base of the weight bag on line with the gully of the 6 cm (2⅜ in) hem. If the curtain is relatively lightweight, a weight may also be needed at the half-width mark. There must be a weight (or weights) in the corners. To get the position correct, fold the hem up and the side turning in (see Fig. 27 (a) page 47 for mitring) by your chosen allowances and poke a soft-lead pencil in between the layers of the interlining to make a mark right in the corner, see Fig. 34. The weight is placed just above and to the right (or left) of the pencil mark. Sew the weights into position.

The interlining at the corner can either be cut away, across the corner, and the sides brought up to create a 'raw-edged' mitre which is cobbled together roughly, or a mitre of the interlining, can be drawn up round the weight, using the same method as described on page 47 and the angled folds stitched together coarsely. The former will give you a less bulky corner; the latter will feel more generous. You can also simply fold the interlining hem up and the side in over the weight and cobble the edge of the side turning down on to the hem. The decision as to which method to use will depend on the weight of both the face fabric and the interlining and the finished effect you want.

Now make the mitred corner for the face fabric layer. Use the method already described, bringing the mitre up round the interlining and adjusting it until the edges fit together well. You will find it easier if you use a fine, metal knitting needle rather than your fingers to do some of the adjusting, see Fig. 35. Ladder stitch the angle of the mitre, as already described. When the mitre is finished, use a blunt knitting needle to make sure that the interlining is well

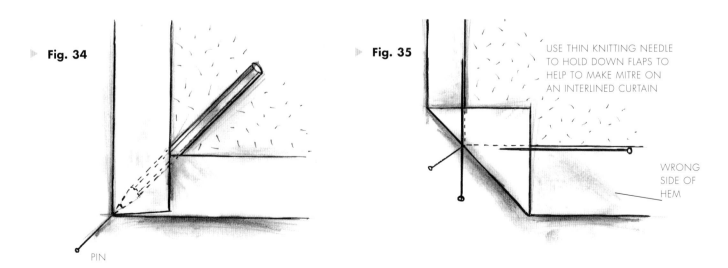

Fig. 34

PIN

Fig. 35

USE THIN KNITTING NEEDLE TO HOLD DOWN FLAPS TO HELP TO MAKE MITRE ON AN INTERLINED CURTAIN

WRONG SIDE OF HEM

stuffed into the corner of the face fabric mitre.

Fold the rest of the hem up – face fabric and interlining together – making sure that the interlining is well packed down into the gully of the hem. Use a blunt knitting needle or a strong length of cardboard. Herring-bone stitch the hem up, using really strong thread, taking up a stitch of fabric from the interlining above the raw edge of the hem and all but the face layer of the fabrics of the hem. With face fabrics which fray badly, it helps if the raw edge is zigzagged or the hem allowance increased by a sufficient amount to allow you to turn the raw edge in. Hemming a curtain is very much easier if it is weighted with a brick, or secured with bulldog clips, at each end of the area you are working on.

Serge stitch the 4 cm (1⅝ in) side turning, making sure that you do not stitch above the baseline for the proposed heading. As with the hem, the interlining must be well packed into place in the fold of the side turning – use a blunt knitting needle to help you. Make sure that the stitching in the area of the mitre is firm, but not overworked, because stitching which is too tight in this area distorts the hang of the mitred corner.

Take the appropriate lining and, with the seams aligned, and the hem of the lining 2 cm (¾ in) above the hemline of the curtain, smooth it into place right side up over the already worked curtain.

Interlock the lining to the interlining, using the same method of folding back as you did for the interlining. Lining should be locked in place on the seams and at the half-widths, with an extra line of interlocking 15 cm (6 in) in from the side turning of the curtain to give extra durability. The lining should have a bridge of 'Virginia Twist' (page 48) between it and the hem.

Cut off any excess lining material on line with the fold of the side turning of the curtain. Fold in the lining by 2 cm (¾ in) and slip hem the lining in place down the side turning. Once again you will be able to do this work much more quickly if you weight the material at either end while you are working on it. The slip-hemming of the lining should start (or end) about 5 cm (2 in) along the hemline, making sure that the stitch at the corner above the mitre is worked twice and the first (or last!) stitch two or three times to ensure durability. This is the area of out-and-out hardest wear for a curtain, so make sure that it is firmly stitched and knotted.

Measure off the tabled section of the curtain to the finished length, marking the measurement with pencil and drawing a straight line between the marks.

Cut off the lining and the interlining, using the pencilled line as your guide. Be extremely careful not to cut the face fabric. Fold the face fabric down and over the raw edge of the cut lining and interlining, and secure the fold with pins inserted head up. Trim the face fabric so that it will fit under the proposed heading tape.

Fold up the edge of the curtain, as for the lined-only curtain (see page 50), by quarter widths, and pull the result carefully back to the edge of the table so that you can continue to work on the rest of the widths, section by section, until the curtain is finished and one side matches the other.

The application of the heading tape is the same as that for lined-only curtains (see page 50).

Iron or press the curtain, lining first, then face fabric, using spray starch to restore the glaze if necessary (don't forget to cost in the spray starch!). Fold and pack according to the instructions on page 126.

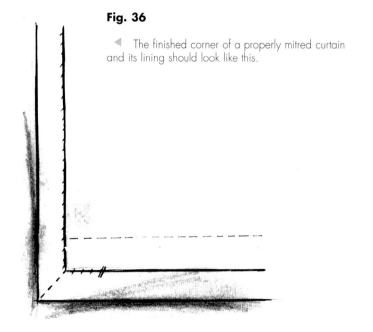

Fig. 36

◀ The finished corner of a properly mitred curtain and its lining should look like this.

HAND-HEADED, INTERLINED CURTAINS

This type of curtain has to have its size, widthwise, calculated so that it is made up sufficiently wide for the subsequent pleating to take up just the right amount to make the curtain fit the track correctly. It is wise to work this out in advance to ensure that you have sufficient material. Stripes are difficult to deal with for hand-headings because the stripes often do not work in neatly with the necessary measurements for the pleats and spaces. The instructions and formulae for 'mapping' hand-headings are on page 64 and fortunately these do not involve any complicated sums! Do your 'mapping' and cut the face fabric to size if necessary. Then follow the instructions on pages 54–55 for hand-made interlined curtains until the side turning has been serge-stitched.

The standard method of construction for hand-headed curtains is to continue with the making up described on page 64 until the lining has been slip-hemmed down the side turning. Then fold the top of the lining back slightly so that you can measure and mark the interlining. Draw a straight line across the marks. Cut off the interlining, using the pencilled line as a guide. Be extremely careful not to cut either the face fabric or the lining at this stage.

Smooth and flatten both the face fabric and the lining upwards and away from the cut interlining, and cut off both the face fabric and the lining together to give an allowance of 4–5 cm (1¾–2 in). Bring the *lining* forward and down to expose the cut top of the interlining, leaving the face fabric undisturbed.

Cut off a length of the heading buckram (preferably fusible) sufficient to deal with all the widths of curtain you are making up, plus a bit extra.

Fold the end of the heading

Fig. 37

▼ (a)

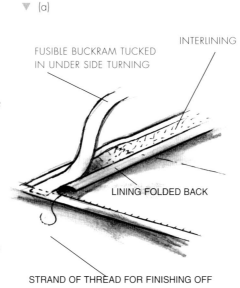

FUSIBLE BUCKRAM TUCKED IN UNDER SIDE TURNING

INTERLINING

LINING FOLDED BACK

STRAND OF THREAD FOR FINISHING OFF

▼ (b)

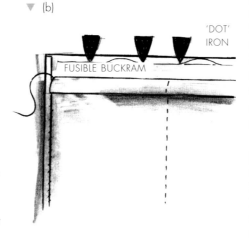

'DOT' IRON

FUSIBLE BUCKRAM

buckram over by the same amount as the side turning allowance and tuck the folded end of the heading buckram into the side turning between the layers of interlining, with the top of the buckram lined up with the cut edge of the interlining. See Fig. 37 (a).

Bring the trimmed face fabric down over the heading buckram and press only the face fabric into place by 'dotting' the iron tip at intervals so that the glue of the fusible buckram melts and it, together with the interlining, becomes fixed in place. See Fig. 37 (b). Fold the side turning in to a neat angle before dotting it. This dotting is necessary because if you ironed all of the face fabric down, you would not find it easy to insert the needle when hand slip-stitching the lining into position. Be very careful not to let the tip of the iron touch the heading buckram during this process – the glue melts on contact and the consequent mess on the iron is a nightmare to remove.

Fold the lining under so that the fold line is 1 cm (⅜ in) below the heading. The folding and measuring must be very precise and straight because when the hand pinch pleats are sewn into place, the lining must be even on either side of the pleat. Slip-stitch the lining into place along the fold and then iron all the layers so that the fusible buckram holds everything neatly. The stitches must be small and very neat, so this is time-consuming work and explains why curtains with handmade headings are expensive.

The curtain is now ready for the pleat and space measurements to be marked off. Do this with pins inserted, head up, along the length of the heading. As you will already have mapped the size of the curtain, this measuring off is very simple. Instructions for making up hand-headings are given on pages 64–65.

AN ALTERNATIVE METHOD FOR MAKING HAND-HEADED, INTERLINED CURTAINS

This alternative method is neat, time-saving and, with practice, quite easy.

Cut and join all the lengths of fabrics in the usual way and make up the curtain so that you are putting together

Fig. 38

▷ (a)

WRONG SIDE

LINING

FACE OF CURTAIN

with all the proper processes, only the face fabric and the interlining. Pin or tack the interlining (untrimmed) in position at the heading to prevent it slipping and distorting. When this part of the making is complete, turn the whole curtain over so that the right side of the face fabric is uppermost.

Lay the prepared lining with the wrong side up on the face of the curtain, making sure that seams lie on seams and that the lining hem is 2 cm (¾ in) above the hem of the curtain.

Measure off the finished length and pencil a line to serve as a guide for the machine-stitching with which you will work this type of heading. Pin all the layers together firmly and frequently. Trim the lining at the side so that it is the same size as the fold of the side turning and then fold 2 cm (¾ in) of it back on itself. This 2 cm (¾ in) fold will become the fold for the side turning of the lining, see Fig. 38 (a).

Pin the lining down the sides and along the hem, for safety's sake, and then move and measure the rest of the widths, dealing with the heading area as described above. Trim the sides of the lining at the other end of the curtain and fold it in the same way as above, see Fig. 38 (b). Make sure that all the layers are pinned together and that the pins are inserted for subsequent easy removal.

▷ (b)

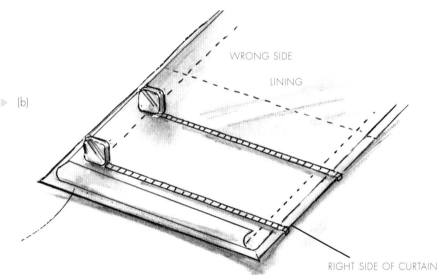

WRONG SIDE

LINING

RIGHT SIDE OF CURTAIN

Take the curtain to the machine. Open out the side turning so that it is flat and machine the top from the raw edge, using the pencilled line as a guide and keeping the fold to the lining in place at both ends, see Fig. 38 (c). Do not forget to open out the further end before machining across it. Take the curtain back to the table. Remove all the pins. Work at a long side of the table and spread out the curtain so that the top faces you and the interlining is uppermost, see Fig. 38 (d). With extreme care cut the excess interlining away as close to the machine stitching as you can manage.

Trim the face fabric and the lining back to 5 cm (2 in) and pull the lining out gently from under the curtain. At this point it will be hanging down on the floor. Iron the 5 cm (2 in) seam open.

Measure off a length of fusible buckram sufficient, plus extra, for your needs and 'middle it up'. This means that you should start the process of application fairly close to the middle of the heading area, bringing the face fabric part of the 5 cm (2 in) seam over and 'dotting' it in place with the iron. Make sure that the edge of the fusible buckram is packed really close against

Fig. 38 (continued)

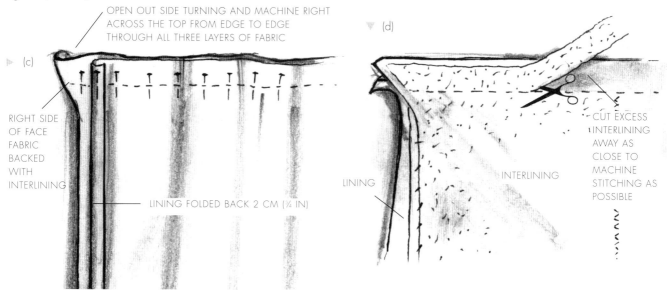

OPEN OUT SIDE TURNING AND MACHINE RIGHT
ACROSS THE TOP FROM EDGE TO EDGE
THROUGH ALL THREE LAYERS OF FABRIC

(d)

(c)

RIGHT SIDE
OF FACE
FABRIC
BACKED
WITH
INTERLINING

LINING FOLDED BACK 2 CM (¾ IN)

CUT EXCESS
INTERLINING
AWAY AS
CLOSE TO
MACHINE
STITCHING AS
POSSIBLE

LINING

INTERLINING

the gully of the 5 cm (2 in) face fabric
seam. Fold the end of the buckram to
fit and tuck it in under the side
turnings, cutting off any excess
buckram. Tuck the face fabric back
down the side turnings so that the top
in that area is neatened. Using a
knitting needle helps with this.

Bring the lining material up ready to
be 'dotted' into position over the
fusible buckram. Take care to ensure
that you can just see the minutest bit of
the face fabric along the top line before
you finally iron and fuse all the layers.
Do this, too, by 'dotting' before you
iron.

The curtain is now ready for
interlocking but, with this method, the
interlocking must be done horizontally
at intervals of about 50 cm (20 in)
across the width of the curtain.

Construct Virginia Twists (see page
48) individually at the correct points
along the hem (on the seams and at
each half-width).

Slip-stitch the lining to the side
turnings.

The curtain is now ready for the hand-
headings to be made, see Fig. 38 (e).

(e) The top of the curtain should look like this.

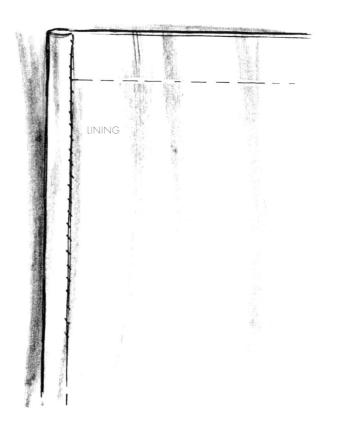

LINING

MAKING UP A LINED-ONLY CURTAIN FOR HAND-HEADING

There are several different ways to make up a lined-only curtain for hand-heading.

The first is to follow the alternative method of making curtains for hand-heading (page 59), omitting the necessary processes for attaching the interlining.

For the second method, follow the instructions for a lined-only curtain (page 50) until the corners have been mitred, but make sure that you leave an open space at the top of the side turning for the insertion of the heading buckram. Fold back the lining and measure off the finished length of the curtain, pencil marking the wrong side of the face fabric and drawing a line to guide the exact placement of the buckram. Trim the top allowance back to 5 cm (2 in). Measure off the length, plus extra, of buckram required and fold in one end to the width of the side turning to strengthen and reinforce

this part of the curtain. Slip the fold of the buckram into the side turning with the top of the buckram on line with the pencilled guideline. Fold the 5 cm (2 in) face fabric allowance over the buckram and 'dot iron' it into place.

Position the lining correctly, trimming the top to a 4 cm (1⅝ in) allowance. Interlock the lining and face fabric. Fold the 4 cm (1⅝ in) top allowance under to leave 1 cm (⅜ in) of the face fabric showing, and slip-stitch the lining carefully and evenly into place. Iron the length of the top to fuse the buckram. Slip-stitch the side turnings of the lining. The curtain is ready for the construction of the hand-headings.

The third method is quick and easy, and really a bit of a cheat. Allow extra fabric at the heading: add 5 cm (2 in) to the width of the heading buckram, see Fig. 39 (a). Follow the instructions for a lined-only curtain (page 50)

until a straight line has been drawn across the pencilled measuring marks. Measure off the required length of buckram, fold one end and place the lower edge of the buckram to the pencilled line with the folded end just slightly in from the side turning. Measure off 5 cm (2 in) above the top line of the buckram and cut any excess material away. Fold the 5 cm (2 in) allowance down over the top line of the buckram and 'dot iron' it in place. Now fold the fabric and the heading buckram forward and down so that the buckram is enclosed in the materials, see Fig. 39 (b). Iron all the layers to fuse the buckram.

This method is attractive from the point of view of speed of making up (and it is, of course, the only way heading buckram can be applied to an unlined curtain), but it does mean that face fabric is visible at the back of the curtain.

Fig. 39

▼ (a) Make sure that the fusible buckram is folded double in the overlap area. This will ensure that the heading does not collapse.

▼ (b) Fold the fabric and buckram forward and down so that the buckram is covered.

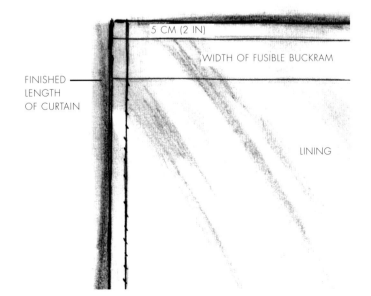

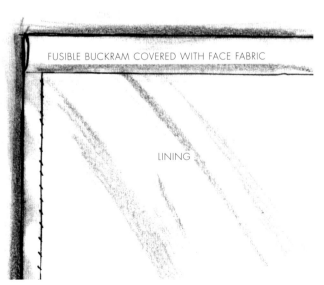

'BALLOON' LINING FOR LINED-ONLY CURTAINS

Balloon lining is a method by which the lining is attached to the side turnings by machine. It is less easy than it sounds and not as quick as you might imagine. The problem is that it is almost impossible to interlock the lining in place so this is a technique which is really only suitable for the construction of small, short curtains.

The measurements for face fabric turnings, hems and linings should be as shown in Fig. 40.

With the wrong side of the face fabric uppermost, press the side turnings in and the hem up.

Fold right-angled mitres at the corners of the hem, attaching weights, as for lined-only curtains (page 50). Pin the mitres into place.

Slip-stitch the hem of the face fabric. Machine the hem of the lining.

Smooth the curtain on to the table right side up with the lining right side down on top of it. Make sure that the seams, if any, are aligned. The lining

must be positioned to have the hemline 2 cm (¾ in) above the hemline of the face fabric curtain. Pin it into place for safety's sake. Fold the sides of the lining to be the same size as the folded sides of the main fabric curtain. Cut off the excess lining along the line of these folds.

Bring the raw/selvage edge of the main fabric and that of the lining together, making sure that you keep the hemline of the lining at the 2 cm (¾ in) mark where it meets the angle of the mitre. Machine these edges together, leaving a long tail of thread at the mitre end to use for hand-sewing the mitre together later.

You will find that you have a sort of fabric 'tube' in which the lining is smaller than the face fabric. Turn this tube inside out. Iron or press the side turnings so that either the raw edges face towards the middle of the curtain, which will give a thin, hollow edge, or the raw edges face back into the fold of

the side turning which will make the mitre at the bottom slightly odd on the inside but which will fill the hollow edges of the turning. The second method will look better against the light and will feel better to the hand. Ease the needle inside the tube gently so that you can catch stitch the face fabric to the lining as close as possible to the seam – wide apart herring-bone stitch will work well. This line of catch-stitching is needed to prevent the lining separating from the face fabric which would make the curtain hang badly.

Ladder stitch the mitres.

Catch stitch the hem of the lining for 4–5 cm (1⅝–2 in) along from the mitre.

Make Virginia Twists (page 48) every quarter-width and on the seams.

Measure off for the finished length of the curtains. Fold and trim the top as usual and apply the desired heading tape.

▼ **Fig. 40**

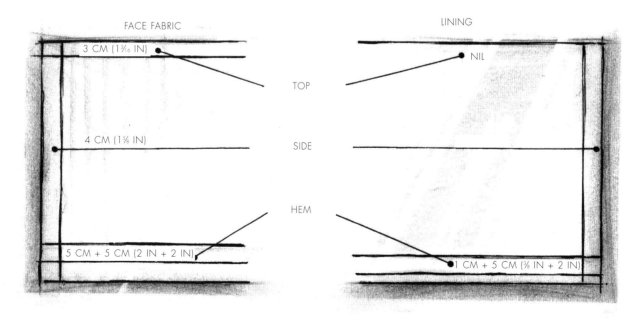

FACE FABRIC

LINING

3 CM (1³⁄₁₆ IN)

NIL

TOP

4 CM (1⅝ IN)

SIDE

HEM

5 CM + 5 CM (2 IN + 2 IN)

1 CM + 5 CM (⅜ IN + 2 IN)

UNLINED CURTAINS AND NETS

Simple, washable curtains and nets are unlined. Whatever fabric is used, it is necessary to cut away selvage edges to relieve the material of a tightly woven edge or the print/colour code which is often printed on the selvage edge of a patterned material.

On patterned material any seams will have to be run-and-fell seams and it is preferable to use hand-stitching on the folded-in edge because this looks much better than machine-stitching which will show at the front. The side turnings can, however, be machined; make them to a finished width of about 1.5 cm (⅝ in). The hem should be a 2 cm (¾ in) plus 6 cm (2⅜ in) fold which can be machined straight across, or slip-hemmed in place.

On net curtains, which are difficult to handle in making up because the material is slippery, you must be sure to use a thread which is compatible with the fibre of which the net is made. Otherwise you will have problems with puckered machine-stitch lines. Puckering can be much reduced by using a long strip of paper under the seams/turnings as you machine. Use a roll of cash register paper, available from office supply shops. Tear paper away after machining. Remember that you must triple or even quadruple the track measurement for net curtains to ensure that they are generous enough. You can trim any seams either with a very neatly machine-stitched French seam (page 48) or trim the seam back to 1 cm (⅜ in) and zigzag the raw edge. The side turnings can be machined or hand-sewn – the former is stronger and neater. Nets get very blown about if the window is open.

When making net curtains, try to get the weft threads of the turnings on line with one another; if they are out of

alignment, the side turnings will look wavy. The hems should be wider than usual – say, 10 cm (4 in) – and double-folded 10 cm (4 in) plus 10 cm (4 in) as this looks much neater. Machine stitch the hem in place straight across from side to side.

The suspension for net curtains can be lightweight tape or a casing with expanding wire threaded through.

The order of sewing for unlined curtains is:

– Seams joined and trimmed
– Side turnings folded in and sewn
– Hem folded up and sewn straight across measure for finished length
– Trim top
– Apply/make chosen heading

DETACHABLE LININGS

Detachable linings can be made in the same way as an unlined curtain, but cut to be narrower than the face curtain by 3–4 cm (1³⁄₁₆–1⅝ in). They are useful if a temporary blackout is needed or, made in insulating material, can be attached to curtains for a window exposed to hours of hot sun in summer. If the curtains are closed during the day, the room temperature is substantially reduced.

VELVET CURTAINS

It is sometimes difficult to decide which way up to have the nap of a velvet material. If the nap is downwards, the colour will be less intense but the material will not catch the dust so much – and vice versa!

Be very careful to remember the necessity of marking the chosen top with a notch as you cut. Zigzag or preferably bias hind the hem before stitching it in place. The hem of a

velvet curtain will sit much better if you slip-hem down between the two layers of fabric rather than along the top.

Velvet 'travels' when the seams are being machined so it is essential to pin before sewing. Machine stitch down the nap. All the hand-sewing must also be done down the nap – hand-sewing against the nap would make the fabric hang very badly indeed.

SPECIAL HEADINGS – HANDMADE

Triple French pleat and goblet are the two most frequently requested types of hand-heading. Both have the same basic construction. What makes this sort of heading more difficult to tackle than those using commercial heading tape is that it is necessary to calculate the disposition of the pleats and spaces. I found this task a nightmare until I hit on my patent method, which I call mapping. It does not involve serious mathematics and it is very reliable provided you bear various points in mind.

You will need a strip of paper about 10–15 cm (4–6 in) wide, and 30–50 cm (12–20 in) longer than the proposed finished width of the heading. Greaseproof paper, such as that used between the layers of fusible buckram heading tape, is very suitable.

The basic formula is the measurement of the curtain return plus the measurement of the track from one end to the end of the crossover point (half of the track). To this measurement add ease – 10 cm (4 in) on biggish curtains and 4–5 cm (1⅝ in–2 in) on smaller ones. Calculate ease at roughly 5 cm (2 in) of ease per 1 m (yd) of curtain track. If you are making handmade triple French pleats

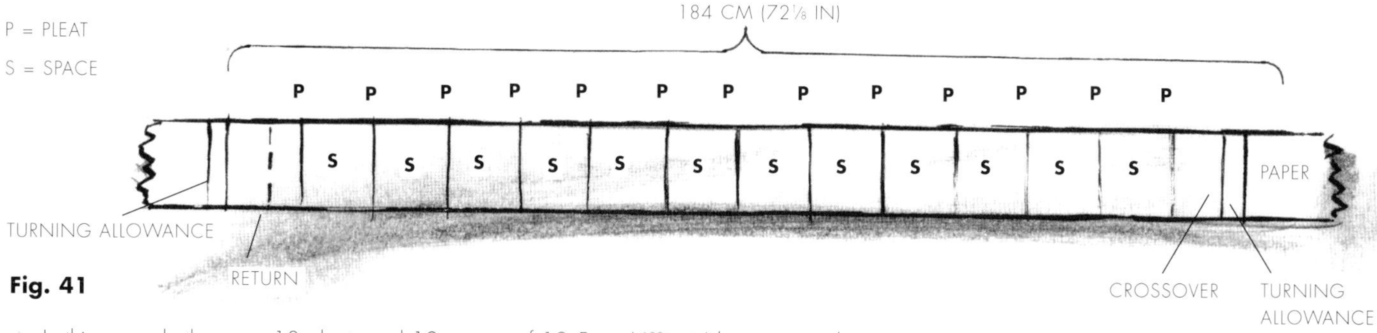
P = PLEAT
S = SPACE
184 CM (72⅛ IN)
P P P P P P P P P P P P P
S S S S S S S S S S S S
PAPER
TURNING ALLOWANCE
RETURN
CROSSOVER
TURNING ALLOWANCE

Fig. 41

In this example there are 13 pleats and 12 spaces of 12.5 cm (4²⁸⁄₃₂ in) between each one.

or goblet pleats as the heading for a pelmet/valance, you do not, of course, have to add in an ease allowance.

AN EXAMPLE IS:

Return	7 cm	(2¾ in)
Half track	166 cm	(65⅜ in)
Ease	10 cm	(4 in)
	183 cm	(72⅛ in)

The total will be the finished width for the heading of one half of the pair of curtains.

You will now have to work out how wide the fabric will have to be to allow for the pleats and side turning allowances. Bear in mind that the spaces should not be more than 10–12 cm (4–4¾ in) wide and the pleats should take up 15–17 cm (6–6¾ in) of material. It is very difficult to arrange a striped material to fit into a handmade heading so that the stripes, pleats and spaces all look correctly disposed. Spaces which are too wide will sag and also pitch too far forward of the pleats which looks very ugly.

Leaving a space at either end of the strip of paper, mark off a length of (in this case) 184 cm (72⅛ in). To each end add the turning allowance you have decided to use – say, 4 cm (1⅝ in). Cut the strip off at these 4 cm (1⅝ in) marks. Now mark the return allowance; 7 cm (2¾ in) and 4 cm (1⅝ in) on from that draw a vertical line to mark the placement for the first pleat which should match up with a hole on the endstop of the track. At the opposite end draw a second vertical line 12 cm (4¾ in) in from the turning allowance mark – this is for the second pleat, which will be placed on the first glider behind the crossover arm of the track.

Without creasing the paper, bring the first and second pleat lines to lie on top of one another and crease the resulting fold. Fold the doubled paper carefully between these two marks so that you have lines which are equal in width but not less than 10 cm (4 in) and not more than 12 cm (4¾ in) wide, give or take 5 mm (³⁄₁₆ in), see Fig. 41.

The strip of paper shows 13 pleats are required and each pleat will need 15 cm (6 in) of fabric. (You cannot make a decently folded triple French pleat with less than 12 cm (4¾ in) of material and more than 15–16 cm (6–6⅜ in) can really only be used if the curtains are very large and bulky, so aim at an allowance of 12–15 cm (4¾–6 in) for the pleats.)

Your next sum is:

Finished width	184 cm	(72⅛ in)
4 cm (1⅝ in) turning allowance x 2	8 cm	(3³⁄₁₆ in)
13 pleats x 15 cm (6 in)	195 cm	(76¹⁹⁄₃₂ in)
Total width of fabric required	387 m	(151²⁹⁄₃₂ in)

The total is the width to which you should cut the main fabric. If, however, the fabric width and the width you require are only a few centimetres (inches) out in either direction, then expand or reduce the amount of material you take up in the pleats. Do not change the size of the spaces.

This method of 'mapping' can be used in many other situations, such as to work out box pleats for a pelmet valance or a bed base valance.

You will have to combine these instructions for measuring for triple French pleats with those for the making up curtains with hand-headings (page 64).

TIP

If you are using Velcro to suspend a pelmet or valance, staple the hook side to the pelmet board and stitch the velour side to the fabric. Hook velcro is difficult to sew on by hand. The name is derived from 'velour crochet'; in French 'crochet' means 'Hook'.

GOBLET PLEATS

Goblet pleats are really very simple to make and they give a beautiful heading which is especially effective in a plain fabric and trimmed with knotted rope or a covered button. They are not, however, really suitable for use as a heading for a curtain which is intended to be drawn. The goblets are too bulky and 'stack back' to be wide. They are better used for 'dead drops' and pelmets.

This type of pleat usually requires 10–12 cm (4–4¾ in) of fabric but the measurement depends upon what is used for stuffing. Short lengths of pipe insulating foam, notched in four places at the base to create a shape like a champagne flute, make a very neat, durable goblet pleat which is also light-weight, see Fig 44. Polyester wadding or tissue paper can also be used as stuffing, but cotton wool or kapok is too heavy since quite a lot is required.

The method for calculating the width of fabric required is the same as that for triple French pleats – use the strip of paper again!

SEWING HANDMADE HEADING PLEATS

Make up the curtain following the methods described on pages 64-65.

The paper strip will show how much space to have between the pleats and how much material is needed to take up into the pleats. Put pins in (head up for easy removal) along the top of the curtain, marking the points of separation between space and pleat, see Fig. 42 (a). I usually cut the paper to give me a 'space' section to use to measure off the spaces, and then cut another strip of paper to the length required for the pleats and use that to measure them off. Do not forget to mark the returns. For the second curtain do the marking in reverse or mirror image, of course.

Fig. 42

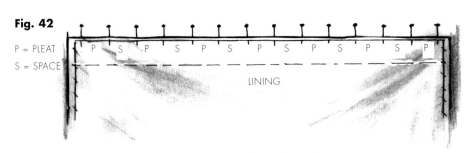

P = PLEAT
S = SPACE
P S P S P S P S P S P S P
LINING

▲ (a) Mark the top of the curtain with pins, inserted head upwards.

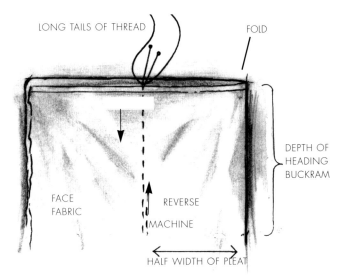

LONG TAILS OF THREAD   FOLD

▶ (b) Use thread that matches the colour of the face fabric when machining the pleats in place.

FACE FABRIC   REVERSE   MACHINE

DEPTH OF HEADING BUCKRAM

HALF WIDTH OF PLEAT

▽ (c) Bulldog clip the triple French pleats after folding them down.

Check your sewing machine for stitch length and tension, and change the colour of thread to match the face fabric if necessary.

Prepare your curtain for presentation to the machine. It may be big and heavy and if you do not get it presenting well, you will find the pleats being pulled off course by the sheer weight of the materials. Present the curtain to the machine wrong side up.

Once you are comfortably seated,

take the right-hand side of the curtain heading and make a fold down the middle of the first pleat section. Do not make this fold too sharp if you are making goblet pleats and do make sure that the top of the curtain is exactly aligned back on itself to ensure that the pleats do not come out 'stepped'. Leaving a nice, long tail of thread, for use later, machine down the length of the buckram, taking the stitching just into the un-buckrammed part of the heading and then reversing back to reinforce the stitching, see Fig. 42 (b). A marker made of masking tape placed at the correct distance away from the machine needle helps to indicate the half-width size of the pleats.

When all the pleats are machined,

take the curtain back to the table, flinging it down and arranging it so that the pleats face you at the long side of your table and just over the edge. Secure the curtain at either end with bulldog clips and check that the width, now that the pleats are in place, is correct. Pull all the long threads to hang down tidily from the pleats, see Fig. 42 (c). Use your fingers and a heavy knitting needle to open out the spine of the pleat from the inside. Now take the curtain material below the pleats and straighten it, so that the fullness of the pleat becomes evident and the warp/weft of the material will hang correctly.

For triple French pleats hold the top, folded ridge of the pleat between

your fingers and, standing sideways to the table, push it downwards gently towards the spine and at the same time bring the side folds up until you can feel and see that you have three equal-sized pleats, see Fig. 43 (a). The centre pleat is usually marginally shallower in depth than the outside ones. Use a stubby knitting needle to ensure that the fabric to the inside of the pleats is sharply down – just pull the point of the knitting needle strongly along the base of each fold. Snap a bulldog clip on to the folded pleat, see Fig.42 (c). and repeat these processes until all the pleats are ready for hand-stitching.

Use a long, strong darning needle and the tails of thread to secure the

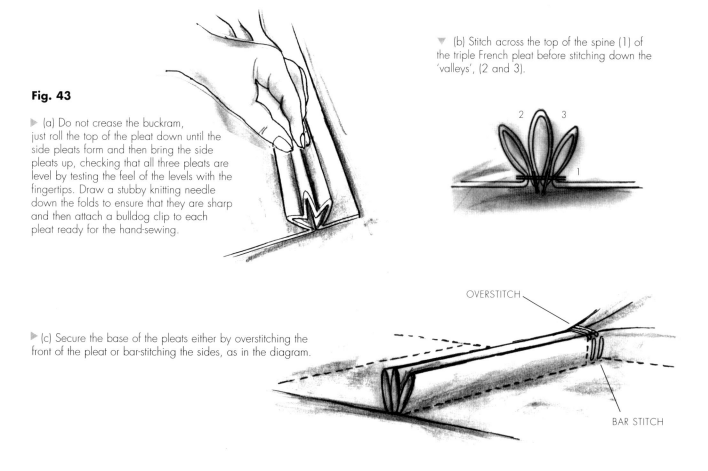

Fig. 43

▶ (a) Do not crease the buckram, just roll the top of the pleat down until the side pleats form and then bring the side pleats up, checking that all three pleats are level by testing the feel of the levels with the fingertips. Draw a stubby knitting needle down the folds to ensure that they are sharp and then attach a bulldog clip to each pleat ready for the hand-sewing.

▼ (b) Stitch across the top of the spine (1) of the triple French pleat before stitching down the 'valleys', (2 and 3).

▶ (c) Secure the base of the pleats either by overstitching the front of the pleat or bar-stitching the sides, as in the diagram.

OVERSTITCH

BAR STITCH

'valleys' of the pleats. Overstitch the top of the spine to reinforce it and give two or three firm stitches to each valley before knotting off and taking the tail of the knot up into the fabric before cutting off, see Fig. 43 (b).

Thread a strong needle with doubled thread and set about securing the base of the pleats. Do not try to sew through the buckram – make the bar of stitching just below it. Choose whether to overstitch the front of the pleats or bar-stitch on the sides. The pleats look less 'strangled' when bar-stitched. Think about using a contrast colour for this job because the contrast thread could be a decorative subtlety.

For goblet pleats follow the same method as for triple French pleats until the pleats are triple-folded. Just take

the tails of thread, and oversew the top of the pleat, knotting off and hiding the tail of the knot as before.

Cut lengths of pipe insulating foam to be 2–3 cm (¾–1³⁄₁₆ in) shorter than the pleat (it should, of course, have been made to take the diameter of the pipe insulating foam which can be adjusted by taking a sliver out of the side if necessary). Cut four notches, about 2 cm (¾ in) long, in the base of the insulating foam, see Fig. 44 (a).

Insert the cut insulating foam in the goblet pleat, making sure that it is concealed. If the top of the foam is cut at an angle and covered with contrast fabric, the stuffing can become a decorative feature which is attractive if the curtains are to be hung at a fairly low window where the goblets can be

seen, see Fig. 44 (b). Pinch the material carefully just below the buckram to make a tiny French pleat which looks rather like the neck of a cracker – the middle pleat will always have a wiggle in it, but this does not matter. Sew only the front of the pleat, see Fig. 44 (c). If you take the stitching round and round the pleat from the spine, you will make the whole pleat jerk forward and the curtain will hang badly.

SUSPENSION

If the curtains are not too heavy, a pin hook is sufficiently strong to suspend them. Do not insert the pin hook into the stitching of the spine – it would very soon break the stitches – but place it just to the side of the spine.

Fig. 44

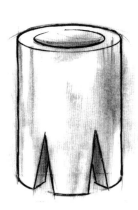

◀ (a) The four notches in the base of the pipe insulating foam will give a champagne flute-shape to the goblet pleat.

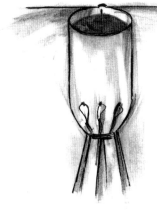

◀ (b) Stuff a shaped foam cylinder down each pleat, making sure that the notches rest about 1 cm (⅜ in) above the base of the buckram.

▶ (c) Do not strangle the neck of the goblet when oversewing it – it will tip forward if you do. Keep the oversewing to the front of the pleat.

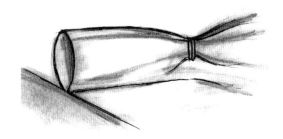

SEWN-ON BRASS HOOKS

Heavy curtains will need 'sew-on' brass hooks set with the head of the hooks 2 cm (¾ in) below the top line of the heading. Preferably use linen or buttonhole thread for this job as it is stronger. The hooks should be sewn on to a length of heavy twill heading tape and positioned to match up with the position of each pleat, see Fig. 45 (a), plus any extra hooks necessary to hang the leading and window edges of the curtain correctly.

You will also have to sew on a band of lining material to cover the base of the hooks (because the hand-stitching looks untidy). Do this by tucking the baseline raw edge of the band under the twill heading tape and sewing both the baseline of the tape and the baseline of the band to the back of the curtain at the same time, using a small running stitch, see Fig. 45 (b). This is tough, time-consuming work for which you should charge per hook and by the hour for the time you estimate it will take to apply the covering band.

HAND-GATHERED HEADINGS

The usual rules for estimating quantity apply, though hand-gathered headings generally need a more generous allowance than usual – up to three times. The top of the curtain should be padded out with a band of heavy duty vilene or interlining. Use a heavy duty thread – preferably nylon, polyester or linen – a metre (yard) longer than the finished width of the curtain. Make a really big knot.

Mark the stitching points with pencil dots – experiment a bit first to find out how far apart the dots should be to achieve the required look (with stripes it may be self-evident).

You will need several lines of gathering, but the number will depend upon the required depth of the heading.

Use a stab stitch into and out of each pencilled dot, making sure that you take up all the layers of fabrics, see Fig. 46 (a). Start a new row of gathering every half-width and pull the gathering up as you go along – this is much easier and much less of a strain on the threads than trying to pull up several widths at the same time. Pack the gathering up as tightly as possible – it can be released to the correct size later.

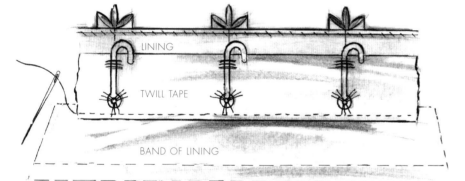

LINING

TWILL TAPE

BAND OF LINING

Fig. 45

◁ (a) Hand-sew the brass hooks to heavy twill tape, spaced to line up with each pleat (or about every 10 cm (4 in) if the heading has been hand-gathered) and with extra to carry the curtain overlaps. Use small running stitches to apply the base of the tape and the covering band in one operation.

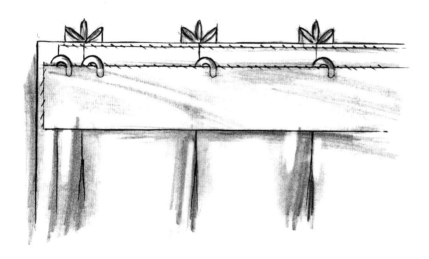

◁ (b) Bring the covering band up and fold the top to be in line with the top of the twill tape. Sew the band and the tape to the lining in one operation, reinforcing the stitching on either side of the hooks for strength.

Anchor the gathering threads by knotting them off securely once the finished width has been achieved.

With the wrong side of the curtain uppermost and the heading jutting over the edge of the table, use bulldog clips to secure the work. Sew heavy duty tape to the back of the gathering, using the tape to keep the pleats in place. If you are using sew-on brass hooks, the stitching can be concealed under the tape, see Fig. 46 (b).

Hand-gathered heading is very time-consuming and you must charge appropriately for the hours it will take.

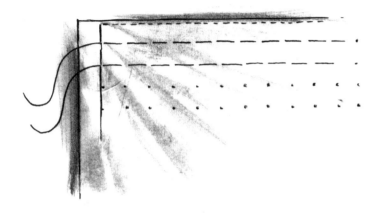

Fig. 46

◁ (a) Use a stab stitch with about 1.5 cm (⅝ in) between each insertion to make the gathering.

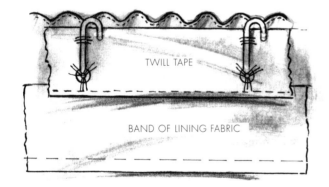

TWILL TAPE

BAND OF LINING FABRIC

◁ (b) Hand-sewn brass hooks and twill tape with a band of lining secure the positioning of the pleats as well as providing the method of suspension.

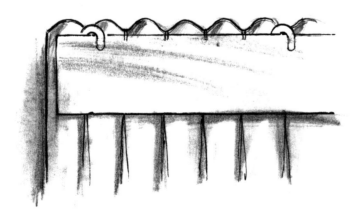

◁ (c) If preferred, omit the hand-sewn hooks and use pin hooks instead.

6

VALANCES
AND PELMETS

The word 'valance' usually means something which is short and gathered and it is confusing because the word is often used to describe a covering for a bed-base. The word pelmet always means a covering for the heading of curtains and it is usually thought of as being hard and flat. I differentiate between the two by referring to a 'pelmet valance' when I mean something soft and headed and a 'hard pelmet' when I mean just that.

The pelmet is, usually, the part of the window treatment where you can begin to indulge in creative artistry!

Basically, a pelmet valance is a short version of a curtain. But, as always, how you make it will be governed by how you are going to hang it up. There are many different types of specialist tracks designed to enable you to suspend pelmet valances in many different ways. Looking through catalogues will give you lots of ideas and, gradually, you will gain the experience to know which ones to use. Double (sometimes triple) tracks work very well, but they do not solve the problem of light showing at the top of the curtain unless they are top-fixed to the ceiling. The classic pelmet board and track will mostly serve you very well. Self-adhesive Velcro (reinforced with staples) stuck to the front of the pelmet board makes suspending a simple pelmet valance very much easier and the recently introduced integral loop Velcro heading tapes have revolutionized the

▲ Despite their curved tops these curtains maintain a level hem. This is achieved by making a template of the top curve and 'exploding' it.

hanging of gathered pelmets.

Any of the available commercial heading tapes can be used to gather the heading of a soft pelmet valance. You can give pelmet valances handmade triple French pleats, goblets, box pleats or cased headings. More ambitiously, you can use a combination of techniques such as ruched bands bordered with contrast piping and a gathered 'skirt' underneath. Ideas and techniques can be combined as you gain experience and confidence. Spend an hour or two trying out ideas and techniques using offcuts and bits and pieces for your experimenting. Figs. 47, 48, 49, 50 and 51 show the diversity of possible treatment.

MEASURING UP AND FABRIC ESTIMATING

The width of a pelmet board and fabric estimating must be considered when you are measuring up. The standard depth is 15 cm (6 in) because this comfortably accommodates the track and the 'stack back' of the curtains.

Fig. 47

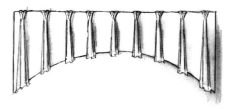

▷ A curved pelmet valance with triple French pleats. The top is treated as if it were a curtain. The hem has to be cut and shaped to ensure that the triple French pleats fall attractively. As the lining of this type of curved shaping will show at the sides, think about having a contrast fabric.

Fig. 48

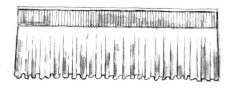

▷ A pelmet valance with a top band, on hessian buckram, which has been ruched between two lines of piping. The skirt is simple, being cut straight and gathered – it would look equally good were the skirt to be curved.

Fig. 49

▷ The same theme as in Fig. 48 but this time the band is flat and padded with polyester wadding to give it a look of plump luxury. The skirt is box-pleated. This sort of treatment is considered to be 'masculine'.

Fig. 50

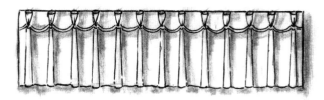

▷ A straight pelmet valance of goblet pleats decorated with swagged and knotted rope. Note that the pleats in this sort of treatment (as in Fig. 47) do not sit on the leading edge of the return, but are positioned 4–5 cm (1⅝–2 in) in from the edge.

Fig. 51

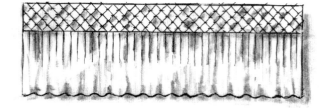

▷ A straight pelmet valance with a smocked heading. This type of heading can also be called 'Tête de Flandres' when you want to impress!

If, for example, there is a boxed-in radiator under the window, the required depth of the pelmet board will be greater. This can result in a deep board! Think, too, about giving the front of the pelmet board a wide curve to accommodate a radiator because this is rather more attractive and less cumbersome. Curtains must be suspended sufficiently far away from the glass of the window to prevent the lining from touching condensation which would make the material rot.

For fabric estimating the same rules apply as those for making curtains but remember to add the return size of the pelmet board to the calculations. I have found that if I am making curtains which require three widths of fabric, I need four widths for a pencil pleated pelmet valance.

The rule of thumb for choosing length is to divide the height of the window into sixths and make the greatest length of the pelmet one-sixth of the overall window length, with tie-backs at one third up from the floor. Such precise proportions are certainly not invariably satisfactory – it is far better to rely on one's eye to judge the best length. If you are not sure, make a paper pattern to the proportion and shape you think might look good and pin it on to the actual pelmet board to see how it looks. If you cannot return to the client's pelmet board, stick the pattern up on your own wall at the height of the client's board.

There are some 'rules', however, which you *must* follow when calculating the size and shape of a pelmet valance – and these apply to hard and soft pelmets, as well as swags and tails and any other treatment. Pelmets *must* be long enough at their shortest point to cover the heading of the curtains and the tops of the windows by at least 10 cm (4 in). If the heading of the curtain is going to be very high up on the wall, the pelmet *must* be even longer than this because the higher the top of a curtain, the easier it is to see underneath it. You *must* note how the window opens – think of the problems of a hard pelmet and an inward-opening window! If there are shutters, check how they open and close; sometimes the sections are small and will not interfere with the pelmet and sometimes the contrary. The proportions and styling you suggest and choose will be dictated by the fabric, the room, the size of items of furniture and the size of the window. Remember not to cut out too much light.

─────── MAKING SOFT PELMET VALANCES ───────

If you are making a straight, gathered pelmet valance, you *can* employ the same method of construction as you use for the curtains underneath, but this will be making a lot of unnecessary work.

LINED-ONLY PELMETS

You can considerably simplify the construction by machining the hemlines of the face fabric and the lining together. The fold of a hem for a straight pelmet valance (with pencil pleat heading tape) should be 5 cm (2 in), and the top turning allowance should be 7 cm (2¾ in). The lining is cut to be 5 cm (2 in) shorter than the length of the face fabric. Join all the widths of face fabric and then join all the widths of lining. Press the seams open.

Put right side to right side and machine the two layers together at the hemline, keeping the seams flat and open. Iron the long seam upwards as you also measure the fold of the hem to be 5 cm (2 in) and iron it into place. Fold in the two ends and slip-stitch them together. Iron down the 7 cm (2¾ in) allowance at the top (as you would for a lined-only curtain), measuring off the finished length of the pelmet valance as you do so. Apply heading tape. This is a quick, easy and thoroughly satisfactory method.

INTERLINED PELMET VALANCE

You can use the same method as above for making up the face and lining layers for an interlined pelmet valance. Cut and join a suitable width and length of interlining (use Domette) and slip it between the layers of face and lining materials so that the bottom raw edge lies in the gully of the hem, see Fig. 52 (page 74). The interlining raw edge should be held in place in the gully of the hem with a line of herring-bone stitching. If, however, you have decided to make up an interlined pelmet valance with the same method of construction as you would use for a curtain, reduce the bulk of the interlined hem by not having the interlining doubled over.

A straight pelmet can have either heading tape or hand-heading, see Fig. 53 (page 74).

Fig. 52

▼ The widths of face fabric are joined. The widths of lining are joined and the hem edge of both are then joined by machine. Insert interlining in the gully of the hem at point A if required, interlocking it in place on the foldline of the hem.

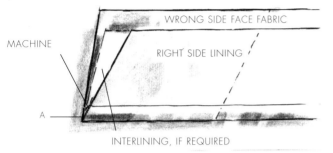

MACHINE

WRONG SIDE FACE FABRIC

RIGHT SIDE LINING

A

INTERLINING, IF REQUIRED

Fig. 53

▼ The finish for a straight pelmet can be heading tape or hand-heading. For tape, make a little pocket to store the cords.

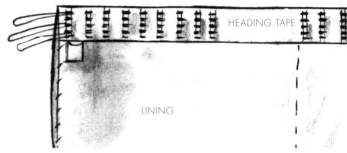

HEADING TAPE

LINING

SHAPED PELMET VALANCE

If you are making up a shaped pelmet valance, remember that the shaping is going to make the lining of the pelmet visible at the sides (this always happens, of course, when material is cut on the cross or semi-cross.) If you feel that the lining will look unattractive, think about using the face fabric as a lining, or a secondary and compatible print, or a contrast coloured lining. It is probably best to use a glazed cotton if the lining is going to be exposed to the sun – coloured lining fabrics sometimes have rather fugitive dyes. Glazed cotton should be used with the shiny side uppermost if the face fabric is also glazed and with the dull side uppermost if the face fabric is not glazed.

Contrast borders which are intended

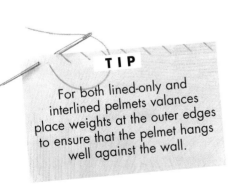

TIP

For both lined-only and interlined pelmets valances place weights at the outer edges to ensure that the pelmet hangs well against the wall.

▲ Here a straight, soft pelmet has been box-pleated and tails have been placed on the returns. The clever use of tags adds further embellishment.

for application to a curved shape must be cut on the cross. If the styling calls for them to be fairly wide, you will probably have to turn up the small hem to both the contrast and the face fabrics so that they lie flat, using

careful herring-bone stitches, and then bringing the shaped lining down to cover the stitching of the hem.

The lining will have to be snipped in places to make it lie properly and the slip-stitching must be done carefully as

it may be visible on the curved sides.

A piped hem looks attractive on a soft curved pelmet and it also makes construction much easier. The piping cord can be removed by pulling it out which will make it less stiff.

MAKING TEMPLATES FOR PELMETS

To start with, design and draw a template for a hard pelmet in a simple shape, such as the one shown in Fig. 54 (a), page 76. Use the back of bargain basement wallpaper, or wall lining paper, to draw the pattern and be very accurate in the measurements because a hard pelmet must fit the pelmet board exactly. If the pelmet is to be very large, you may need to join lengths of paper together with adhesive tape. Measure off a rectangle as shown in Fig. 54 (b), page 76.

You may find a 'flexible curve' (available from stationers) helpful for drawing the curve. Consider the estimated size of the 'stack back' area of the curtain because this needs to be proportionally related to any shaping given to the pelmet above.

You will be making the design 'to the half' – a method frequently used in soft furnishing. Cut out the rectangle to the measured size and then, lining up the lines for the returns, fold the paper in half. Use the measured lines as a guide to draw in, freehand or using a flexible curve, a line to mark the desired curve. Keeping the paper folded, cut both layers of paper together along the curve line. Now open out the resulting pattern to see what it looks like: is it the shape and proportions you envisaged and are they attractive? By adding a little here and paring a little there, would you get something better? Think about changes, but do not make any major ones without consulting your client. If all is well, you now have a template

▲ A pencil pleat valance looks much more interesting with a serpentine top. A shaped board is screwed to the top of the pelmet board and the valance is suspended with Velcro.

which you can use to draw the outline for a hard pelmet.

If you want to make a soft pelmet to the same shape, you will have to 'explode' the template. This is not complicated and it has, in a way, similarities to the 'mapping' used for calculations for the hand-headings (page 64). Try out the technique with paper first.

Take a length of wallpaper and on it measure, from the left-hand side, the length of the return and the full length of the pelmet board. Fold the paper to double the length of the measurements you have just drawn. This folded piece of paper represents widths of material joined to make a length for a gathered soft pelmet.

Cut the shaped template in half. Use one side only. Cut off the return and mark it 'Ret'. Then cut the rest of the halved shaped template into equal-sized strips of 5–8 cm (2–3 in) wide, numbering each strip, see Fig. 54 (c). Move these strips, in correct numerical order, on to the big folded length of paper, and spread them apart evenly.

The return section needs to have a 'space' section of its own size next to it but the other pieces only need to be placed evenly on the paper.

Pin these strips of paper to hold them steady and use the yardstick to draw a line along their top to join them up. Use a freehand pencil line to join the shaped sections at the base. Now remove all the strips and using the pencilled lines as a guide and with the paper still folded, cut along the drawn lines. When you open this pattern out, you will find that you have a very

Fig. 54

▶ (a)

▽ (b) Measure off a rectangle which will show the length of the return, the length of the front of the pelmet board and the depth of the shape at its shortest and longest points.

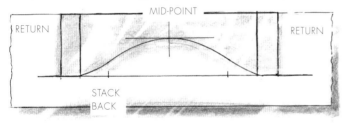

▽ (c) The strips of paper are spread out at an equal distance on the folded length of paper. The cutting line is from the strip marked 9 to the lowest point of the strip marked 2. Cut from lowest point to lowest point, adding seam/turning allowance.

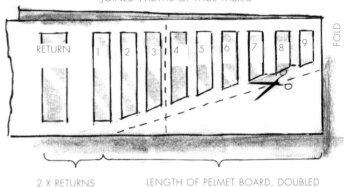

Fig. 55

▽ To make a curved valance with triple French pleats, 'map' the template in the same way as for a curtain heading, spreading the paper strips out to give the required distances between pleats. Note that the cutting of the pleat section is straight at the hemline.

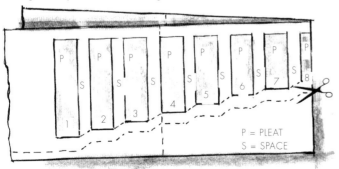

Fig. 56

▽ For an arched window the 'mapping' follows the same principles as above, but with the cutting line at the top. The heading buckram must be cut to the same shape.

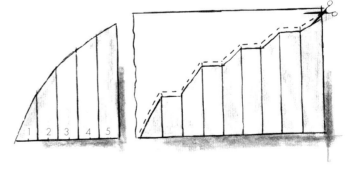

elongated version of the shaped template which you can use (plus allowances) to cut the materials for a soft, shaped, gathered pelmet/valance.

Practise this method several times in paper, using different measurements and shapes, and then move on to trying it out in scrap fabric and putting a heading tape on it. Do not bother to do any fancy tailoring. It now pulls up to the shape you envisaged easily. See Fig. 55.

In adapted forms, this 'exploding' is how to go about making a pattern for a curtain for an arched window, or for a window with an angled top. Just try cutting a quarter circle into strips, spreading the strips apart and you will see the beginnings of a pattern for half an arched window, see Fig. 56.

MAKING HARD PELMETS

Hard pelmets are easy and satisfying to make and look good in formal or 'masculine' rooms. They are often uninspiring in shape and too narrow to be interesting but, with variations, they can be a sensible answer to many problems. For instance, a low bow window is hard to dress attractively if one is nervous of departing from the simplest of straight, gathered pelmet valances, but a hard pelmet with fabric ruched on to it and piping top and bottom could look very neat and attractive.

The standard method of making hard pelmets is to use heavy duty hessian buckram. In most circumstances this is a great mistake because buckram is extremely sensitive to atmospheric changes, especially when installed over a radiator, and it will buckle and distort within a few months of being fitted.

I always use either 4 mm (⅛ in) hardboard or 4 mm (⅛ in) plywood and cut it to shape with an electric saw. These electric saws are readily available from DIY shops and they are worth their weight in gold, enabling even those without well-developed muscles to cut complicated shapes and large quantities with ease. Saws are now available with a vacuum attachment and one which has this useful feature would be a good investment.

To get the shape for a hard pelmet, you have to design and cut out a paper template.

Secure the paper shape to the hardboard or plywood with drawing pins or adhesive tape to keep it steady while you draw round it with a thick pencil. Cut round the pencil line with the electric jigsaw – but please observe every known safety precaution because the saws are dangerous. If you are not careful about keeping the flex well out of the way, the possible consequences are horrendous.

Cut through the return allowances to enable you to make a 'hinge' so that the return of the pelmet can turn the corner round the pelmet board. To make the hinge, you can use heavy duty adhesive cloth tape (but it is expensive), or strips of unpatterned offcuts and rubber-based adhesive to hold them in place. It is helpful to modify the adhesive brush by cleaning it off and then wrapping masking tape around the top of the brush and the handle – this makes the brush smaller and less splayed, enabling you to apply the adhesive neatly.

Making the hinges is not difficult. If you are using hardboard, the rough side should be the front of the pelmet but if you are using plywood, it does not matter which side you use. Take the cut-off returns and, to the back, ram them close up to the middle section of the board, fixing them in position with a strip of adhesive tape or glued offcut. Allow the glue to dry. Turn the rejoined board over so that the front is uppermost and slide the joined return to the edge of the table so that it hangs over at a right angle. Apply a further strip of tape or offcut and slide the result back on to the table. The strip now has a little hump in it and forms a 'hinge'. Do the same to the other end of the board and the result will be the foundation of a hard pelmet with two flaps to be used to go round the returns.

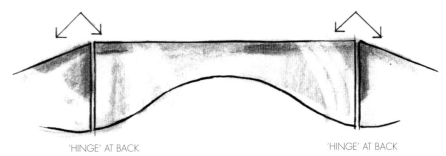

'HINGE' AT BACK   'HINGE' AT BACK

Fig. 57

▲ Make inward-facing 'hinges' at the back.

If you are planning a hard pelmet for a square or angled bay window, you are likely to encounter eventual problems with the face fabric wrinkling unattractively at the angles, which will, of course, be inward-facing. The way to solve this is to make up the pelmet in separate sections for the parts where there are going to be inward-turning angles and then to apply your hinge, made of face fabric, at the back, see Fig. 57. You can also make the hard pelmet with inward-facing hinges, cover it with wadding or face fabric and then stitch the face fabrics down and through the hinges carefully by hand.

Think about how the colour of the board may or may not affect the colour of the fabrics you are going to use to cover it. If you feel that the colour of the board will show through, you could give it a couple of coats of white emulsion paint, cover it with lining offcuts, or glue wallpaper lining paper in place.

To give a plump and luxurious look to a hard pelmet, the face should be covered with a layer of thick bump or polyester wadding – use 50 g (2 oz) or 100 g (4 oz) depending on the look you want. Glue the bump or wadding to the board and cut it to shape after gluing, using the shape of the board as your guide. You will need only dabs of glue but make sure that they are absolutely dry before you apply the face fabric. Hard pelmets without padding look thin and mean.

When you have decided which part of the pattern of the main fabric you want to use centrally on the hard pelmet, cut the widths of material to the depth of the board (plus generous turning allowances) accordingly and ensuring that you use a full width of face fabric to the middle. Because the face fabric is going to be stretched and on display, you must be particularly careful about joining the widths so that the patterns match exactly and the

seams are absolutely straight. Draw a pencil line for a machine line guide, use a much shorter stitch length, trim the seams, iron them open and snip them carefully on the diagonal.

Cut and join the lining, giving it, too, a generous turning allowance of at least 5 cm (2 in). Place the lining and the face fabric right side to right side centring the seams if there are any, and then place the whole pelmet board on top, carefully moving it into position so that both the pattern and the seams

will be centralized from every direction. Now draw lightly with a pencil, round the whole board so that the fabric is marked. Remove the board.

This is the point at which to apply loop Velcro to the heading level of the lining if you have decided that it is desirable. Velcro is helpful for positioning hard pelmets, but it is not strong enough, on its own to suspend the weight, and you will also need to use 2 cm (¾ in) long brass panel pins

▼ Lambrequins – a long-sided version of a hard pelmet without returns – solve the problem of dressing windows on a sloping wall. Velcro is used to attach them to battens placed just within the reveal.

The loop Velcro should be cut to the required length and applied to the right side of the lining which should be folded so that the Velcro is applied to a double layer of fabric for strength. The hook Velcro (preferably the self-adhesive variety) is applied to the front edge of the pelmet board and reinforced with staples gunned into position on the diagonal at frequent intervals. Velcro is expensive, so be sure to cost it in when you work out your estimates.

Place the hard pelmet on the back of the face fabric, wadded side down, positioning it so that the patterns and seams are centralized and the top is on line with the weft grainline. Now apply a good thick line of rubber-based adhesive along the top of the hardboard (avoid the very edge to be sure that it does not flood into the face fabric, and also to make sure that the sewing of the lining will not be affected by the dried glue). Bring the face fabric forward and down on to the glue, starting the work in the middle of the board and working out to the sides to make sure that the fabric keeps to its position on the board. Let the glue dry thoroughly because it is against this top line that you will be tensioning the rest of the gluing.

If you have a complicated pelmet shape, it is wise to reinforce the areas where there will be deep cuts into the face fabric to enable you to bring it round and glue it to the pelmet. Do this with lightweight fusible vilene or short lengths of micropore tape, applied to the vulnerable areas before you cut.

Using the pencilled line as a guide, cut the face fabric to shape along the bottom line, giving yourself a 5 cm (2 in) allowance for pulling up and gluing. Snip the fabric on the convex curves but be very sure to stop short of the pencil line by at least 1 cm (⅜ in).

Paint a line of glue along the

▲ This dramatic lambrequin looks almost like tails at this window. Such a treatment is economical because it does not need very much fabric.

baseline of the hard pelmet, making sure that you do not get glue too close to the edge because that will make slip-sewing the lining into position impossible.

Start in the middle and pull the face fabric up and on to the glue, tensioning the fabric by feel as you go. Work the middle point first, then the point to the right-hand side of that, then back to the left-hand side of it and so on from side to side until the job is finished. You will have to work with reasonable speed to ensure that

the glue does not lose its viscosity. Rubber-based adhesives are user-friendly, however, and you will be able to pull the fabric away from the board if adjustments become necessary later – even days later!

This is the point at which to check that the seams are lying straight.

You will find that the finish is neater if you bring the face fabric up to be a mitre at the corners. This means that you will have to glue the corners up and in – like Fig. 27 (b) in the description of making a mitre for a curtain on page 47 – before applying a bit more glue so that you can bring the 'hem' up and glue it into place. See Figs. 58 (a), (b) and (c).

Trim the side turning allowance if necessary and glue it into position.

Turn the whole board over so that you can check the positioning and tensioning from the front. If all is well, the lining can be applied to the back of the pelmet, turned in and slip-stitched in place neatly along the back edges of the board. Work this slip-stitching so that it cannot be seen from the front and so that there is no sign of tiny pulls to the face fabric. See Fig. 58 (d).

With a little practice, hard pelmets are fairly quick to make and not all difficult.

VARIATIONS

With slight variations the above basic hard pelmet will work well all the time. The variations take the form of shaping and trimming. If the decoration is to be piping, you will have to make it up in advance in lengths which will fit the edges to which it is going to be applied. The ends of the piping should be butted (see the section on crossway strips and piping, pages 84–89). The piping is glued into position along the

top and the bottom edges – piping and rope do not usually look good taken down the sides of a hard pelmet. Please make sure that you do not get the glue close to the hard edge of the board – make the seam allowance on the piping a little wider than usual so this is easier.

Braid can be applied to the face of the pelmet by marking the position carefully after the board has been covered and the baseline stitched – just leave the sides open so that you can slip the raw ends of the braid neatly underneath. Braid can be glued in position by following the marked line very neatly and in such a way that the

Fig. 58

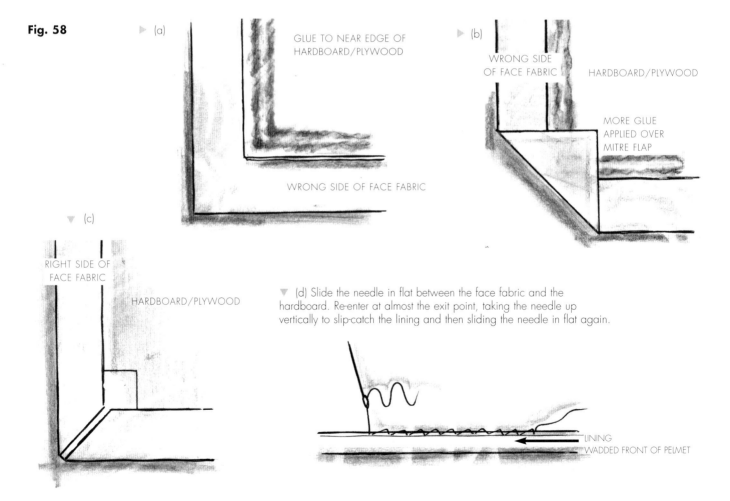

(a) GLUE TO NEAR EDGE OF HARDBOARD/PLYWOOD

WRONG SIDE OF FACE FABRIC

(b) WRONG SIDE OF FACE FABRIC

HARDBOARD/PLYWOOD

MORE GLUE APPLIED OVER MITRE FLAP

(c) RIGHT SIDE OF FACE FABRIC

HARDBOARD/PLYWOOD

(d) Slide the needle in flat between the face fabric and the hardboard. Re-enter at almost the exit point, taking the needle up vertically to slip-catch the lining and then sliding the needle in flat again.

LINING
WADDED FRONT OF PELMET

braid can be brought down on the glue to fix it. You can glue the braid itself, but it is hazardous to control. The glued braid will have to be reinforced by being stitched into place. Do this with a long or curved needle, a strong, matching thread and herring-bone stitch taken from the right-hand side to the left-hand side of the board and underneath the face fabric, see Fig. 59. Glue has a limited life, so do not rely on it holding braid in position without stitching.

Positioning braid round curves and corners must be carefully worked out in advance of gluing. First pin it into position to ensure that the gathering up for curves is correctly positioned, using a matching thread to create the gather by hand and leaving the tail free so that the gather can be pulled up to perfection once the braid has been glued into position. See Fig. 60.

On corners it may be necessary to stitch down the mitred folds of the braid, especially if the braid is quite

thin and loosely woven, see Fig. 61. You will not find this positioning as easy to do as that for curves. If the braid is wide, you may find it best to ladder stitch the mitres.

Rope can be obtained with a flange already attached. This makes it easy to apply to the top and baseline of a hard pelmet. Apply it in the same way as piping, but first unpick 5–8 cm (2–3 in) of the flange at each end, then untwist the rope, flatten the separated strands and secure this flattened end

Fig. 59

▷ A long, fine darning needle or a large curved needle is the easiest to use for applying braid to a hard pelmet. By using a herring-bone stitch worked from right to left under the braid you will be attaching both sides of the braid in one operation.

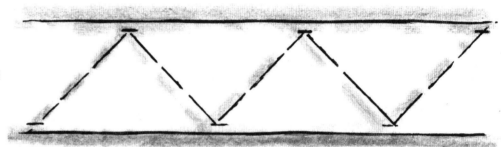

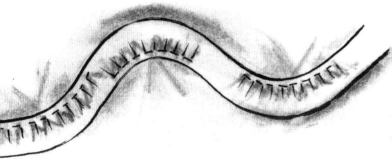

Fig. 60

◁ Use a matching thread to make little gathering stitches which are pulled up to make braid fit and lie neatly on curves.

Fig. 61

▷ Make sure that all the mitres face in the same direction when applying braid to a hard pelmet.

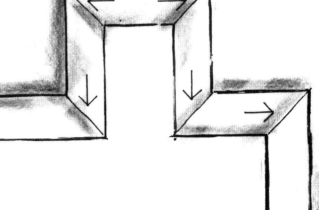

with micropore tape before tucking it under the edge of the board and covering it with the lining. Rope applied to the face must be applied in simple designs, otherwise there will be too much pulling and tension from the hand-stitching.

A contrast-bound edge to the heading of a hard pelmet is best applied by hand. Do this with a width (joined if necessary) of fabric cut on the straight and sufficiently wide when folded in half down its length to make the contrast edge and to turn this under to the back of the pelmet. Use a small, neat running stitch down the gully of the fold and on line with the required depth of the contrast to hold the strip in place. The flap of the fold is brought down to cover the stitching which, once gently ironed, will not show. Use the same method, but with a folded strip of bias-cut fabric, to contrast-bind a simple, shallow curved edge.

SUSPENDING A HARD PELMET

This is not difficult though, if the pelmet is large, it is probably a two-person job. The Velcro will assist with primary positioning but, as already mentioned, this suspension will have to be reinforced. Use brass panel pins 1.5–2 cm (⅝–¾ in) long if you use plywood as the base and use copper hardboard pins of the same length if you used hardboard. Make sure that the pins are all cleaned of the mineral oil used by the manufacturer to preserve them (or you will get indelible, black marks on the fabric).

▶ This straight, hard pelmet has been generously wadded to achieve the unusual deep buttoned effect. It provides an impressive frame for the window-seat.

Work the point of the panel pin carefully through the angle of a weft and warp thread of the fabric as close to the top of the board as possible. Hammer it almost home at an angle (so that it acts like a sort of hook), see Figs. 62 (a) and (b). Then, very gently and using the point of a large safety pin, wiggle the hole about to close it, see Figs. 62 (c) and (d). It will be virtually invisible. Use a space between the stitches of the seam lines where possible, or hide the panel pins under trimming if it is suitably positioned.

The panel pins need to be used at intervals of about 15 cm (6 in), to carry the weight of the board but it is only on extremely large and extremely heavy boards that the wall sides might have to be nailed down on to wooden battens.

Fig. 62

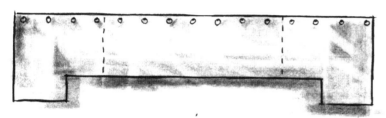
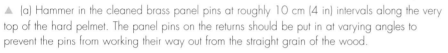

▶ (d) Work the hole back together again over the head of the panel pin with your fingers.

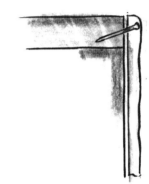

▲ (a) Hammer in the cleaned brass panel pins at roughly 10 cm (4 in) intervals along the very top of the hard pelmet. The panel pins on the returns should be put in at varying angles to prevent the pins from working their way out from the straight grain of the wood.

PELMET BOARD

▶ (b) Side view of the insertion of the panel pin. Stop hammering just before the head goes through the fabric.

PULL MATERIAL FORWARD WITH POINT OF SAFETY PIN

◀ (c) Use a safety pin to pull the fabric forward of the head of the panel pin.

▶ This study has been decorated in toning fabrics. The hard pelmet has been quilted.

CUTTING AND APPLYING BIAS-CUT STRIPS

There are several methods of cutting and joining bias-cut strips for contrasts and piping. You need to know about the quickest!

If you are cutting strips to make piping, they will need to be wide enough to give you two seam allowances and the correct amount to fold around the piping – a No. 6 piping cord, which is quite thick, will need more allowance than a standard piping cord. Standard workroom piping cord needs bias strip to be cut to a width of 5.5 cm (2⅛ in). Be careful and accurate about cutting bias strips, and also about joining them, because the final look of your work will be much improved if the piping is properly constructed. To have the joins on bias strip facing in different directions is a sin in soft furnishing terms!

Pin a small piece of material around the piping cord you plan to use.

Pretend that the pin is a line of stitching just underneath the piping cord. Measure off a 2 cm (¾ in) seam allowance and the resulting width will be correct to fit the piping you are using.

As far as possible avoid using very short lengths for bias strip – it looks untidy and unprofessional.

On cushions and loose covers, bias strip gets very hard wear so do make sure that you use a sufficiently substantial fabric and a strong sewing thread. If you are making up all your piping in advance, make sure that you use a matching thread for the machining. It is difficult to hide the stitching of pre-made up piping.

The fibre content and weight of the fabric you use for the bias strip must be of the same quality as the face fabric to which it is being attached. Remember the old rule: dull face fabric, use the dull side of a glazed cotton uppermost;

shiny face fabric, use the glazed side of the cotton uppermost.

Reduce the length of the stitch on the sewing machine when machining the bias-cut strips together. The stitch needs to be short so that the seam does not open into tiny gaps when the bias is turned around the piping cord.

If you are so low on fabric that you have no alternative but to cut the strips on the straight, this is acceptable, but there will be problems with puckering on curves and corners.

CUTTING BIAS STRIP

The rough guide for fabric estimating is that 50 cm (20 in) of material will give about 9 m (9¾ yd) of bias strip. Take a piece of fabric as wide as you judge to be necessary to produce the quantity of bias strip you require and fold it in half on the diagonal. Cut through the diagonal fold. Turn the

Fig. 63

▽ (a) 5.5 cm (2⅛ in) is the width for bias strip intended for standard piping cord. This gives two seam allowances of 4 cm (1⅝ in) and 1 cm (⅜ in) to go round the cord.

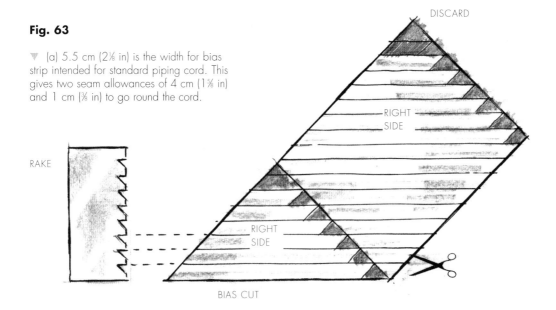

fabrics so that both are wrong side up and the diagonal fold faces you along the length of the table. Pin or weight the material so that it does not move around. Mark the fabric to the required width using an appropriate 'rake' to do so, see Fig. 63 (a). Mark the fabric at frequent intervals because this makes cutting very much easier. You can cut as many as four layers of fabric at once, which saves a lot of time.

Trim the strips by cutting the ends, on the straight of the fabric, so that all the strips have their ends cut in the same direction, see Fig. 63 (b).

Pile all the strips on top of one another, disbursing the various differences in length throughout the pile, and take the pile to the sewing machine to commence joining them. Keep the pile on your knees while you are doing this work.

Use a short machine stitch to join the strips right side to right side, see Fig. 63 (c), feeding the seaming under the foot without lifting it. You will get

metres (yards) and metres (yards) of looped strips which can then be cut apart.When you reach the cutting apart, drop the strip wrong side up into a box, dribble-folding it as you go so that it is the correct way up and unravelled ready for using. This dodge, which can also be used to control the strips of fabric used for frilling, saves hours of time and muddle. It is not necessary to iron the seams of bias strip – just open them out and finger-press them as you go along when inserting the piping cord.

INSERTING CORD INTO BIAS STRIP TO MAKE PIPING

Make sure that the piping cord is pre-shrunk. If you are uncertain about this it is wise to boil the cord, tied into a loose hank, for 5 minutes. Dry it out on a wire tray in a medium oven for about 30 minutes.

If the cord has a very pronounced look of rope to it (which may show

through the covering fabric as lumpiness), you can remove some of the lumpiness by pulling the cord hard, down its length, over the edge of the table.

If your machine has a cording foot, this is the foot which should be used for this job. (If you are sewing professionally, you should have a machine which takes a cording foot.) If you have not yet got this facility, use the zip foot and adjust it so that it will stitch close to the cord. Use thread

▼ (c) Join bias strip in one continuous operation by feeding the bias ends under the machine foot without lifting it. Cut the strips apart when the joining has been completed.

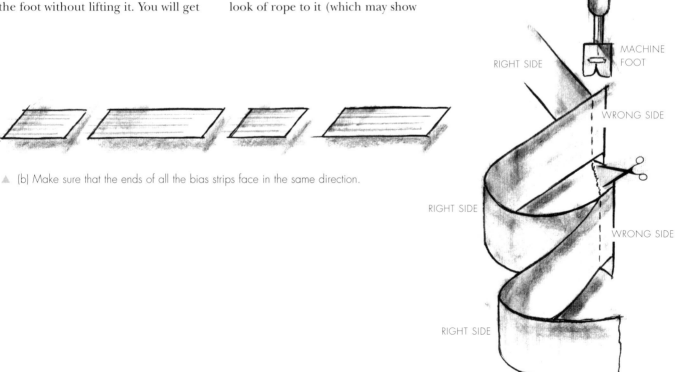

▲ (b) Make sure that the ends of all the bias strips face in the same direction.

which matches the colour of the material.

Fold the joined bias strip with the cord inside the fold, so that the raw edges are even, and secure the cord in place with machine stitching on the right side of the fabric and next to the cord. This job is quick and easy if you have a cording foot – slow and dreary otherwise.

Piping can be applied directly to the item it is being used to trim. This is the quickest and neatest method because it avoids too many layers of machine stitching.

If you have a cording foot you will be able to machine stitch a layer of face fabric, a layer of frilling, a layer of piping and a layer of lining all in one operation. This takes a bit of organizing and a good deal of careful pinning but it can be done, and, of course, with only one line of stitching there is far less puckering.

Where piped cord is to be inserted into another seam, such as the joining points on a loose cover, the cord should be pulled up and through the bias strip for the required length, cut off, see Fig. 64 (a), and then pulled back into the bias so that the bias becomes 'empty', see Fig. 64 (b). If the seam allowance is 2 cm (¾ in) you should cut off 3 cm (1³⁄₁₆ in) of cord to ensure that it is well out of the way of any forthcoming stitching. This simple dodge can be used in many different circumstances – the eye is deceived into thinking that the cord continues on into the seam. Application is as shown in Figs. 64 (c) and (d).

When applying piping cord to curves, especially very sharp curves such as those on tie-backs, the seam allowance of the bias strip will have to be snipped at suitable intervals. On a very pronounced curve these can be as close as 7 mm (¼ in).

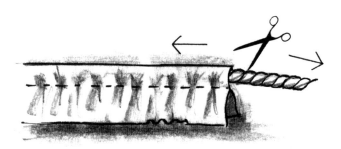

Fig. 64

▲ (a) Pull the cord out of the bias strip casing and cut off the required amount to 'empty' the casing.

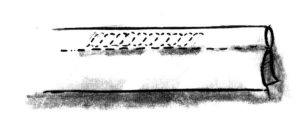

▲ (b) Pull the cord back into the bias.

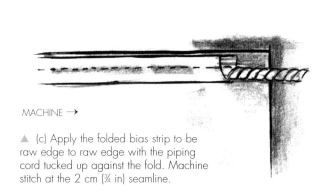

MACHINE →

▲ (c) Apply the folded bias strip to be raw edge to raw edge with the piping cord tucked up against the fold. Machine stitch at the 2 cm (¾ in) seamline.

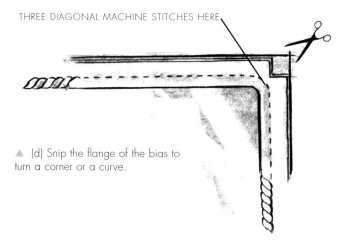

THREE DIAGONAL MACHINE STITCHES HERE

▲ (d) Snip the flange of the bias to turn a corner or a curve.

CUTTING AND JOINING THE PIPING CORD

There are several methods for cutting and joining the piping cord.

METHOD 1

This is the standard method. Unless it is done very carefully the results can be lumpy and bumpy as well as time-consuming.

Cut the cord so that the ends overlap by about 4 cm (1⅝ in).

The cord usually has three twists to it. Cut about 2 cm (¾ in) off one of the twists on one side and the same off two of the twists on the other. This gives you a total of three twists which can be 'woven' back together to re-form the cord and oversewn firmly. See Fig. 65.

METHOD 2

Lay the two ends of the cord side by side and cut them through on the diagonal, see Fig. 66 (a). Use 1.5–2 cm (⅝–¾ in) wide 3M micropore tape and cut a piece about 4 cm (1⅝ in) long, see Fig. 66 (b). Lay the two cut ends of the cord on to the edge of the sticky tape so that the diagonal ends abut and then roll the tape around the cord, see Fig. 66 (c). This makes a very neat join.

Fig. 66

▼ (a)

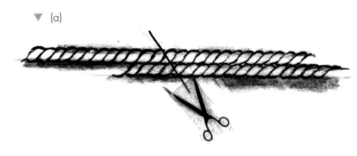

▶ (b)

MICROPORE TAPE

▼ (c)

Fig. 65

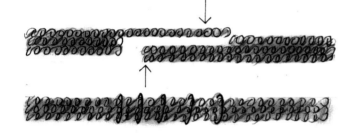

Fig. 67

▼ Leave an open working space to deal with the fiddly jobs of joining the piping cord and the bias.

START MACHINE STITCHING HERE

RIGHT SIDE – BASELINE

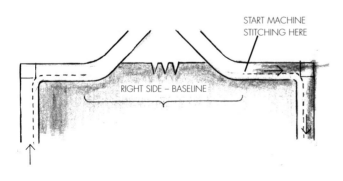

─── REJOINING THE BIAS STRIP AROUND PIPING CORD ───

There are two methods for joining bias strip and it depends what you are making as to which once you choose. I would use Method 1 in a place where the join will be hidden – on, say, the piping in a bed-base valance – and Method 2 for the piping on, say, a silk cushion.

Whichever method you choose, it is necessary to start and finish the application of the piping by giving it a free end about 15 cm (6 in) long and beginning and ending the machining so that these free ends will overlap comfortably and leave you clear working space. You must also give yourself enough unstitched space when starting to machine the piping into place to enable you to manipulate the bias strip and the cord easily when they are joined. See Fig. 67.

METHOD 1

Fold the left-hand side of the bias strip up and back diagonally along the straight of the material. Fold the right - hand side of the bias strip down and back diagonally so that the fold abuts the opposing side exactly, see Fig. 68 (a).

Finger-press these folds firmly and cut away any excess fabric to give a 1 cm (⅜ in) seam allowance. Pin along the fold to make sure that you do not lose track of what you are doing.

Reduce your machine stitch length and machine across the seam of the strip. Open the seam and finger-press it.

Join the piping cord by whichever of

Fig. 68

▼ (a) Fold the bias back on itself so that the folds butt on the straight of the material. Reduce the length of machine stitch to join the bias.

▼ (b) The ends of the piping cord in the diagram have been joined with tape.

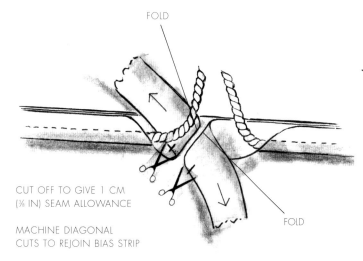

CUT OFF TO GIVE 1 CM
(⅜ IN) SEAM ALLOWANCE

MACHINE DIAGONAL
CUTS TO REJOIN BIAS STRIP

FOLD

FOLD

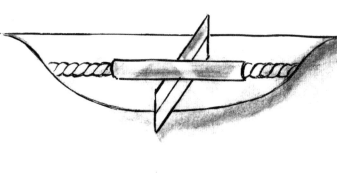

▼ (c) Ease the rejoined cord into the fold of the bias and machine across the gap to close.

▼ (d) This method of neatening bias round piping cord will look very trim if you make sure that the folded overlap is on the diagonal. It is not really acceptable to have the overlap straight. Use this method of joining when the join is not going to show.

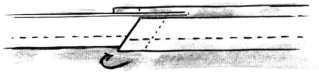

the methods on page 87 you prefer, see Fig. 68 (b).

Increase your machine stitch length. Fit the bias strip around the joined cord, pinning the seam allowance to the face fabric if you feel it is necessary. Pack the cord well back into the folded bias and machine it into place, see Fig. 68 (c).

METHOD 2

Fold the right-hand side of the bias strip back diagonally along the straight of the material and trim to give a 2 cm (¾ in) seam/foldback allowance.

Pin the lower raw edge in place on line with the raw edge of the face fabric, making sure that the fold remains in place.

Trim the length of the left-hand side of the bias strip to a point where it will tuck neatly over the fold of the right-hand side and under the cord.

Cut and join the cord to fit the space using whichever of the methods on page 87 you prefer.

Pin both layers of allowance of the seam allowance of the left-hand bias strip, with the cord inside it, raw edge to raw edge with everything else and ease as necessary to make sure that it is all going to fit together smoothly and neatly, see Fig. 68 (d).

Machine stitch all the layers together along the line of the cord.

RUCHED PIPING

Ruched piping is a useful decorative trim. This type of ruching can only be done with a fairly lightweight material. You will need triple the length of the cord for the bias strip because it must be generously pulled up.

Take a length of piping cord 50 cm (20 in) longer than the measurements of the item you intend to pipe. Tie a knot at one of the ends. Fold the bias (or straight-cut) strip round the cord. Start machining, using matching thread, at the knotted end and every 40–50 cm (16–20 in) stop – leaving the machine needle in the fabric – and carefully pull the cord towards you while pushing the material round the cord away from you, see Fig. 69.

Dispose it evenly along the cord. Continue stitching, stopping, pulling and pushing until the length of cord is completely covered.

Neatening the ends is fiddly. Use Method 2 (page 87) with the underlap flattened out and the overlap folded, on the straight and re-ruched. Carefully done, this join is almost invisible.

Fig. 69

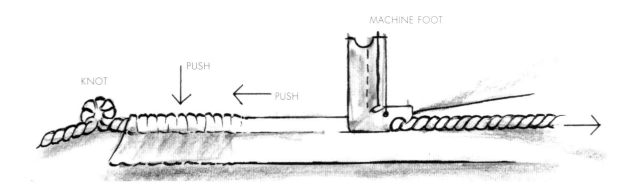

▼ You can use either bias-cut or straight-cut strips to make ruched piping.

KNOT

PUSH

PUSH

MACHINE FOOT

7

TIE-BACKS AND TRIMMINGS

——— TIE-BACKS ———

There are several methods of making tie-backs. The one outlined in this chapter is quick and, carefully worked, very effective. It cannot be used in all cases because the type of material and the shaping of the tie-back may demand another method.

Buckram is the stiffened hessian material upon which a tie-back is based. It comes in varying widths and thicknesses, and you should choose a weight which is compatible with the type of curtain you have made. For example, for heavy, interlined curtains you will need a 'double-starched hessian buckram'. For tie-backs teamed with lined-only curtains I sometimes use a double layer of fusible heading buckram. Buckram is expensive but worth buying in bulk so that you are always sure to have a supply. The 46 cm (18 in) width is suitable for most uses.

▶ Frills have been inserted into narrow bands of the face fabric to make these country-style tie-backs. The blind is made in contrasting fabric in the same yellow and blue.

As with cushion covers, it is necessary to prepare a selection of tie-back templates in a variety of shapes and sizes. Every time you make a new shape, add it to your collection. Mark the templates with their size (length from side to side) and with the length of piping and frilling that they will require.

The technical word for the length of a tie-back is 'embrace' and, ideally, it should be decided after the curtains are actually hung because the length will depend on the form of the window, the depth of the 'stack back' and the drape which the curtain is intended to have. If a post-hanging measurement is not going to be possible, you should look at the window and, bearing your intended treatment in mind, use a soft tape measure to measure the length of the tie-back from the point at which it will hook to the wall to a downward angle at the point where the drape of the curtain will look most attractive in relation to the window. This measurement will have to be doubled because the tie-back is folded

Tie-backs should not be over-long because this looks very ugly and also makes them hang heavily and badly. Curtains which have an unusually wide 'stack back' look better if they are draped over an attractive brass hold-back arm. Rope and tassel tie-backs are adjustable for length by re-tying the knot.

On small windows tie-backs should be narrower in depth than they should be at larger windows where they can be quite deep.

Choose a motif from the face fabric pattern to use in the same position on each tie-back. Because of the way patterns are printed, it may not be possible to have the same motif on both the right-hand side and left-hand side. Make sure all right-hand side motifs match and all left-hand side motifs match.

MAKING A TEMPLATE

Cut an oblong of paper to the overall embrace length of the tie-back – say, 80 cm (32 in) and about 50 cm (20 in) deep. Mark the middle point lightly and next draw a firm line about 5 cm (2 in) to one side of this.

Tie-backs look and hang best if they are curved, so draw such a crescent/banana shape within the oblong and make it the appropriate depth to suit the window you are dressing. Do not curve the ends of the crescent shape too sharply because this makes applying piping rather difficult. The fold point of the tie-back will be the heavy vertical line because the ring at the back needs to be hidden behind the front of the tie-back and the anchoring motif – say, a butterfly – must be placed so that it is to one side of the fold, see Fig. 70, page 92.

MAKING UNPIPED TIE-BACKS

Place the template on the buckram, pencil round it, cut it out and then use the buckram shape to outline the required number of tie-backs. You do not have to worry about reversing these shapes because the buckram can be used either way round. Be as economical as you can with the placing of the templates but be sure to cut the buckram on the straight.

Fill a washing-up bowl with a 10 cm (4 in) depth of lukewarm water. On the table spread a layer of lightweight interlining, big enough to accommodate all the buckram shapes neatly. Have ready a second layer of interlining of the same size. Slide the buckram shapes quickly through the water, shake off the excess and lay the shape on the interlining.

Work quickly, repeating the process until all the shapes are wet and then lay the second layer of interlining on top of the shapes,

patting and smoothing it into place.

Use a hot iron to seal the interlining to the buckram. The magical property of double-starched hessian buckram is that the wetting softens the starch enabling you to use it like glue – it becomes, in effect, fusible.

Allow the shapes to dry before cutting the interlining to shape around the buckram. Do this job as accurately as possible. Leave the shapes flat on the table until completely dry before embarking on the next stage.

Place two of the buckram shapes on the wrong side of the face fabric at the chosen spot of the chosen anchoring motif. Remember that one of the two shapes will be for the left-hand side tie-backs and the other for the right-hand side tie-backs, so you will need to adjust the placement of the shapes to ensure that the motif is in the right position. Pencil lightly round the buckram shapes, mark a meticulous 2 cm (¾ in) seam allowance and then cut them out. Use these two pieces to place and cut all the required number of tie-backs – it is much easier to line up the patterns if you do this.

Linings for tie-backs are dull if they are made of ordinary curtain lining material, especially since many people are lazy and often leave the tie-back simply hanging down, wrong side showing, from the hook on the wall. Think about using a plain, coloured material or some of the face fabric itself . . . it can be randomly used without worrying about pattern placement.

Pin each piece of the face fabric shapes wrong side up to the chosen lining and cut round them, leaving the pins in place so that the two pieces do not become separated.

A simple unpiped tie-back can be machined all round, leaving an opening at the bottom for the insertion of the buckram. Remember to reinforce the machine stitching at the starting and stopping points because there is considerable strain on the opening while the stiff buckram is being inserted. Trim the seams to 1.5 cm (⅝ in) but leave the full seam allowance in place across the opening area.

Make one end of the buckram into a 'rabbit's ear' and slide it into the tie-back case, making sure that the seams are to the back of the tie-back. Wiggle around with a strong knitting needle to achieve this if necessary. Repeat the process with the other end of the buckram. Adjust the tie-back case over the buckram to make it fit properly and then slip-stitch the opening neatly, with small stitches bringing the face fabric over the buckram and folding the backing material under.

Do not worry if the tie-back looks warped at this point. Damping and pressing will remove this and, while the tie-back is still a little warm and damp, lay it out flat weighted with bricks until it is dry.

Apply hollow brass rings – 2.5 cm (1 in) is a useful, all purpose size – as shown in Fig. 71. Do not use plastic rings – they break.

MAKING PIPED TIE-BACKS

Follow the instructions on page 91 for unpiped tie-backs until the lining has been cut out. Prepare the bias strip and piping cord and apply it to the right side of the front piece of the tie-back as shown in Fig. 72.

Cut and rejoin the cord (using Method 2, page 89), and neaten the bias strip (using the same method). Just make sure that the fold to the bias is placed so that it is at the back and base of the tie-back where it will be hidden by the curtain.

On the curves it is wise to machine the little snipped flaps down flat to prevent them from getting caught up during the next stage.

Pin or tack the front to the back, right side to right side, piped side uppermost. Use the stitching of the piping as a guideline. Leave a space open at the bottom to allow for

the insertion of the buckram.

Trim the seams to 1.5 cm (⅝ in) but leave the full seam allowance at the opening. Slip-stitch the opening of the tie-back.

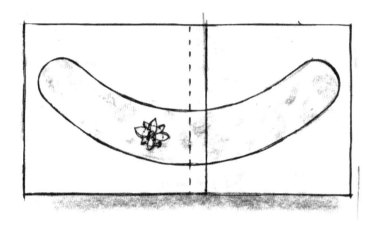

Fig. 70

⬛ The anchoring motif should be placed so that it will be visible when the tie-back is installed. Do not forget to adjust the positioning for the reverse side.

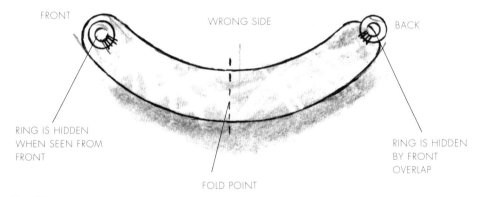

FRONT   WRONG SIDE   BACK

RING IS HIDDEN WHEN SEEN FROM FRONT

RING IS HIDDEN BY FRONT OVERLAP

FOLD POINT

Fig. 71

⬛ Correct positioning of the tie-back rings will ensure that they sit properly on the tie-back hook. Alternate the position of the rings for the reverse tie-back.

MAKING PIPED TIE-BACKS THE CLASSIC WAY

Follow the instructions on page 91 for unpiped tie-backs until the lining has been cut out. Iron the lining up round the buckram to make the seam allowance well turned in – this will help to give a neat finish later. Then remove the lining and set it aside.

Place the prepared buckram shape on the cut-out face fabric and bring the raw edges up and round the buckram, tacking it into position and clipping the fabric, if necessary, to make it lie flat. Place prepared piping round the edge following the instructions above and tacking it into position. Pin the prepared lining into position on the back and then slip-stitch all the layers so that the face fabric, piping and lining are joined. Sew on brass rings as described on page 92.

FRILLED TIE-BACKS

A frilled tieback can have a straight edge to the frill, as shown in Fig. 73 (a), or a curved edge, as shown in Fig. 73 (b). Frilled tie-backs can be made with or without piping.

Frilling is applied after the piping and before the back section. Cut notches on each piped piece to mark the points between which you want to place the frilling and repeat these notch marks on all the other tie-backs so that they will be uniform and balanced. For curved frilling, see the instructions on page 100.

PLAITED TIE-BACKS

Plaited tie-backs are not difficult to make, but they are often constructed so that they look more like plaited loaves of bread – very stiff, bulky and heavy with the ends trimmed with a straight bar of material which clashes with the soft informality of the plaiting.

You will have to experiment a bit,

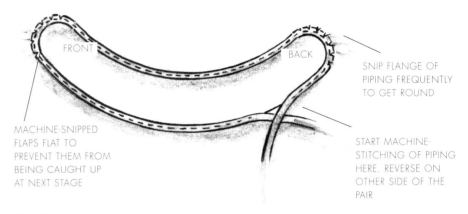

FRONT   BACK

SNIP FLANGE OF PIPING FREQUENTLY TO GET ROUND

MACHINE-SNIPPED FLAPS FLAT TO PREVENT THEM FROM BEING CAUGHT UP AT NEXT STAGE

START MACHINE-STITCHING OF PIPING HERE. REVERSE ON OTHER SIDE OF THE PAIR

Fig. 72

Very accurate cutting and careful machining of the piping cord will ensure a correct finished size. Until you are experienced at negotiating the very sharp curve, it is probably best to tack the piping in place first.

first, to discover how wide a plaiting of three uniform widths of material will be. When you are satisfied with the effect that these three strips of material have achieved, cut strips – at least 1.5 m (60 in) long of double the width plus 4 cm (1⅝ in) for seam allowances.

Turn the strips into tubes. Iron the seams open without pressing the sides of the tubes using a long, thin ironing board. Centre the seam down the back of the tube.

Cut strips of 100 g (4 oz) polyester wadding to a width to match the width of your tube.

Machine the tube and the strip of wadding together across the top of the tube.

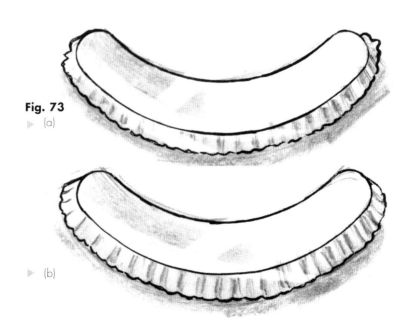

Fig. 73

(a)

(b)

Use your fingers to poke the tube and the wadding back in on themselves, and then use a wooden yardstick to turn it all inside out, see Fig. 74 (a). Done with a little care, the wadding will get itself neatly stuffed into the tube. Cut the machined end off so that the tube is open at both ends.

Make up as many tubes as you will need for the number of tie-backs you are making.

Fold the ends of the tubes in and iron into place. Place three tubes on top of one another so that the folded ends are aligned and then stitch all three tubes together at the same time, see Fig. 74 (b). If you are using three different colours, you should place them in the same order for every tie-back.

Pull the joined ends together by wrapping the thread round and round and between the layers tightly to achieve this shape, see Fig. 74 (c).

If you are feeling very diligent, you could blanket stitch round a brass ring before slipping it along one of the tubes as far as the gathered end, see Fig. 74 (d).

Use a bulldog clip to hold the tubes tense while you do the plaiting. Take care not to be interrupted when you are plaiting because you will find yourself plaiting to a different tension and rhythm if you leave this work and then come back to it. When the plaiting has reached the required length, use a bulldog clip to hold the tubes together. Slip a brass ring down one of the tubes before cutting them to the required length. Turn the ends in and neaten them as described above.

Plaited tie-backs made like this tend to be soft and rather elastic, so you should slip-stitch a strip of folded face fabric down the back to prevent stretching.

Fig. 74

▼ (a) Have the seam uppermost and hold the wadding against the seam as you use the yardstick to turn the tubes inside out.

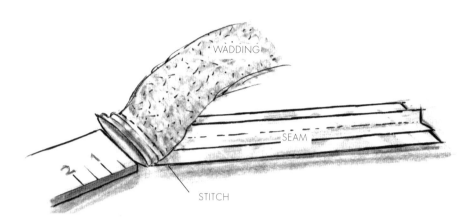

◄ (b) Oversew the ends of all three tubes together, keeping the stitching neat and tight.

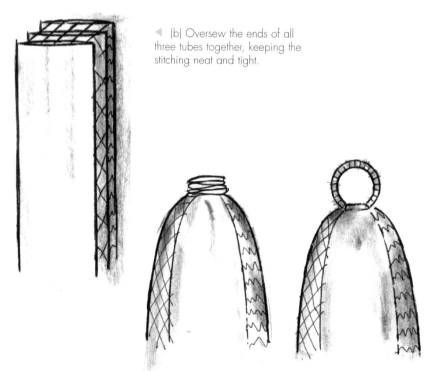

▲ (c) Wrapping a strong thread round and round the top stitching of the tie-back will give the end a pleasing shape. Deal with the other end in the same way after you have done the plaiting.

▲ (d) Blanket-stitching round each brass ring will make your work look very superior. It is worth doing when you want to achieve a top-grade finish. Do not forget to slip the rings in place when you start and finish the plaiting.

GENERAL POINTS ABOUT TIE-BACKS

It is very difficult to trim, pipe or contrast-bind a tie-back with sharply pointed ends, see Fig. 75.

Unstructured tie-backs, such as those made without buckram, break down very quickly and can soon look shabby. This does not apply to plaited tie-backs or to rope.

Rosettes and bows should not be placed right at the end of a tie-back because they can be obscured behind the window edge of the curtain. Place them one-third of the way in from the ends.

Do not demean the work by using cheap hooks to anchor the tie-backs to the wall. Cup hooks are not acceptable! The three styles shown in Fig. 76 look good and work efficiently. Always look for a deep hook. Tie-back hooks have to be screwed into a rawlplugged hole in the wall. The hole should be on line with the window edge of the curtain. The height should be such that the placement of the tie-back enables the curtain to drape attractively in relation to the whole styling treatment and to the window itself.

Tie-back hooks can be very elaborate and expensive. It is really up to the client to decide what to use.

▲ This is a classic crescent-shaped tie-back, made on buckram and piped. The curtain above is softly draped.

Fig. 75 ▶

Fig. 76

▷ Three styles of tie-back hook which work well. Because they have a single screw, they do less damage to walls.

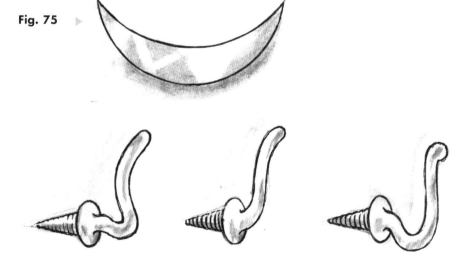

ATTACHING ROPE TO TIE-BACKS, PELMETS, CUSHIONS AND CURTAINS

Rope has a snake-like life of its own and, unless very carefully handled, can twist in such a way that it distorts the item to which it is attached. The other problem is getting the cut ends out of the way.

Rope can be obtained ready-sewn to a flange of tape. It is simply called 'flanged rope' but it is only the more expensive brands that are properly attached so that the rope is not over-twisted. Very stiff rope is difficult to apply and should be avoided for 'soft' soft furnishings though it is fine for upholstery.

You cannot sit in front of a television set and sew rope to a cushion simultaneously! If you did so, you would find that the tension and twist of the rope goes wrong. As with piping, the rope must be longer than the item to which it is being attached. Stand at the table and 'gentle' the rope into place round the cover. The great trick is that the cover should have an opening about 5 cm (2 in) long – in either one of the seams near the bottom of the cushion as this allows the cut ends of the rope to be unravelled and carefully re-spliced so that the join is virtually invisible. The cut ends are then tucked down the opening which is closed with hand-sewing. See Fig. 77.

If you are using flanged rope to trim a cushion, treat it like piping but cut 7–8 cm (2¾–3 in) of the flange free before you start work so that the rope is also free and can be unravelled and re-spliced. See Figs. 78 (a) and (b).

Micropore tape is useful to wind round the frayed ends or to hold the strands flat and tidy. When cutting off a length of rope (or fringe), wind a short length of micropore around the rope

Fig. 77

▼ Sewing rope to the edge of a cushion.

Fig. 78

▷ (a) Re-splicing rope.

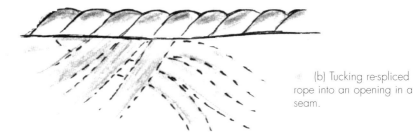

▷ (b) Tucking re-spliced rope into an opening in a seam.

Fig. 79

▼ Attaching rope to a curtain must be done with the curtain laid out flat on the table. Do not 'force' or pull the rope as you attach it, but ease it into position so that the twist does not distort and, therefore, make the curtain hang badly.

MACHINE-STITCHING   HAND-STITCHING

RIGHT SIDE OF FABRIC

at the cutting point and cut through the tape to make a fray-free end.

You will get a much less pulled and dimpled effect to the attaching of rope to a curtain if you make a line of strong-thread machine stitches in a colour that exactly matches the face fabric. Pencil a line on the wrong side of the face fabric – on curtains this is usually about 15 cm (6 in) in from the side turnings because this is the point at which a curtain achieves a natural fold. Use a long machine stitch to stitch down the pencilled line. Do not take rope horizontally along a curtain unless it is very soft – stiff rope will make the curtain hang badly.

Use the line of stitches as a guide for applying the rope and as the 'anchor' for the actual stitching on of the rope. Hand-sew the rope to the machine stitching by catching the thread under every other machine stitch, see Fig. 79. The rope will have to be tucked under the heading tape (hand-sewing the tape in that area) and either taken up and into the hem at the bottom, or finished off in a decorative way such as a whorl or a trefoil.

FRILLING

On big jobs upwards of 1,000 m (1,100 yd) may have to be gathered, so it is essential to find a way to do this job quickly and well.

For certain makes of sewing machine, there are clever attachments, like a special type of foot, which will gather and apply the frilling in one operation. These gadgets work well if you are not also applying piping or a line of contrast colour, neither are the gadgets designed to deal with fabrics which are not fairly lightweight, so they have their limitations.

If the frilling is going to be attached to the face fabric and both edges of the frill will be on display, you will have to resort to the standard method of gathering up with long, loose straight machine stitching. It is very much easier to gather up well if you machine *two* lines of gathering stitch, applied with the fabric wrong side up, and then attach the frill by sewing down the centre between the lines. Remove the gathering stitches by pulling through the bottom thread so that the top stitching can be pulled out easily.

ZIGZAG GATHERING

This method for gathering was such a revelation to me when I was first shown it that I can still remember the thrill of finding out that such a difficult, boring job could be made so easy!

Adjust the machine stitch length to the longest stitch. Adjust the machine zigzag width to a narrow zigzag. If the seam allowance is 2 cm (¾ in), the zigzag should be well within this allowance.

Zigzag at the 1 cm (⅜ in) mark, *on the wrong side,* using the side of the machine foot (often 1 cm (⅜ in) wide as a guide. Start with a couple of zigzag stitches and then stop, leaving the needle in the material. Take very strong thread (crochet cotton is fine) and draw the end under the foot and against the needle. Lower the foot. Zigzag the thread down for the entire length of the fabric being frilled, see Fig. 80.

Gather up by pulling up the thick thread, which you first anchor with a pin to prevent it pulling through.

Fig. 80

⚠ Make sure that the gathering is narrow. If the zigzag is too wide it will stray into the seam line and show.

APPLYING FRILLING QUICKLY AND ACCURATELY

Use zigzag gathering to put in the gathering stitching. Make up, and zigzag gather, all the frilling strip you will need in one fell swoop and cut off what you will need for the job in hand. If, for example, you are putting a frill into the leading edge of a curtain with a finished length of 2.5 m (98½ in), you will need to cut off 5 m (196 in) of the prepared strip. Neaten the ends if necessary. Follow the diagrams in Figs. 81 (a), (b) and (c).

Anchor the strong thread at each end by winding the thread round a pin. Using a fine knitting needle at the points where the strip is pinned down, pull the strong thread upwards in a loop so that the strip becomes gathered. Wind the loop around the pin to hold it. Continue from end to end until all the material is gathered, adjusting the gathering so that it is evenly disposed between each pin and inserting further pins if necessary.

The pins should be inserted so that the heads will be to the left of the sewing machine needle and removed as you go along. Place the extra pins well back from the machine stitch line, leaving only those which have the thread looped round them in their original place. This avoids having to do too much stop-start machining as only the pins with the loops have to be removed while sewing.

On curtains the frilling on a leading edge should have the lining material brought to the stitching line of the frilling. With great care, and a lot of pinning, the line *can* be machine-stitched in place down the leading edge – the potential problem is getting the tension and positioning correct. Otherwise you should slip-stitch by hand.

Fig. 81

▶ (a) Mark the mid- and quarter points on the edge of the fabric to which the gathering is to be attached (which should be right side up). Mark the mid- and quarter points on the zigzag-gathered strip which is to be gathered up.

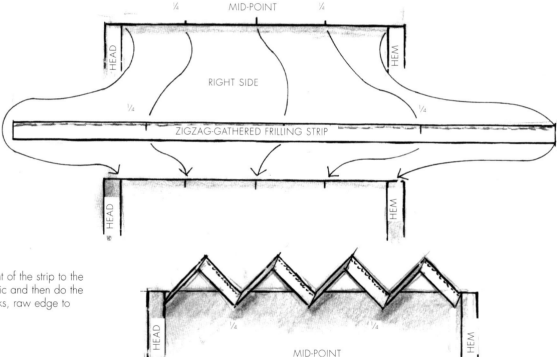

▶ (b) Match the mid-point of the strip to the mid-point on the main fabric and then do the same with the quarter marks, raw edge to raw edge.

▶ (c) Bring the mid-points of the strip down to the mid-points between the marks, then pull up the gathering.

▲ A scarf tie-back has to be tied to the front each time it is used,
so may not be suitable for curtains that are drawn every day.

GENERAL POINTS ABOUT CUTTING AND PREPARING STRIPS FOR FRILLING

Make sure that the strips of fabric for frilling are cut very accurately. Use an appropriate 'rake'. Uneven cutting will cause problems.

Cut across the width of the fabric on patterned materials, so as to keep the pattern the right way up. Plain materials, such as glazed cotton, can be cut down the length.

As the strips are cut, pile them on top of one another so that the pattern of each piece faces in the same direction. In the finished article the pattern should face upwards on the horizontal and outwards on the vertical.

Join the strips in the same way as for bias strip (page 84). It is not necessary to pattern-match the seams for frilling although it is sensible, of course, to try to make the patterns reasonably compatible at the joining point. Close up, it looks crude to have a dark green leaf next to a bright red flower, though this will be less apparent in the gathering. If there is a section in the design which is very emphatic, test it for effect when roughly gathered up to see what happens. Sometimes such patterns can 'block' so that the frilling will have a section where that part of the pattern looks very heavy. This will be especially evident if you have joined a strip to another of the same pattern – you should jumble the strips to avoid this.

If you have decided to use main fabric on both sides of the frill as in Type 2 (page 103) and assuming that you are having a contrast-bound edge, make sure that the pattern faces outwards on both sides towards the contrast binding.

Once joined, snip the strips apart, trim and iron the seams if necessary and then 'dribble fold' them into a box. You may have three different

lengths of strip to deal with – for example, a patterned fabric for the front, a bright blue for the contrast binding, and bright yellow for the backing. Dribble fold each section into a separate box and place the boxes in a position where you can sit at the machine and pull all the layers out of their boxes easily as you are sewing them. Work out the direction and the way up you will need each section when collating them for feeding through the machine. If they are the right way up and out to bring to the machine easily and in a flowing, unravelled state, you will save yourself hours of time and confusion.

After the component parts of the strip are joined, they will need to be ironed so that the eventual frill will be very neat and crisp. Pin the raw edges together at 50 cm (20 in) intervals to prevent fabric travel and drag when you zigzag gather. It will not matter if you find yourself with little pleats appearing as you zigzag gather.

Once zigzag-gathered, you will be able to cut off the lengths you require as you need them, neatening the ends in a way which is compatible with the work you are doing.

To curve the frilling into a seam, pull the strong thread back through the zigzag by about 20 cm (8 in), cut the released section at a long angle from the raw edge towards the fold, see Fig. 82 (a), and then use the strong thread to make a gathering stitch by hand up the newly cut edge, see Fig. 82 (b).

To get the width of a contrast binding really even is difficult without a cording foot. The width of contrast binding can be adjusted by using different thicknesses of piping cord and a cording foot of an appropriate size to fit it. Sew all the layers together at one time with the cord sandwiched into the contrast binding and being pulled out as you go along. This is another dodge which will save you hours of time and also much aggravation.

Generally you will need double the

Fig. 82

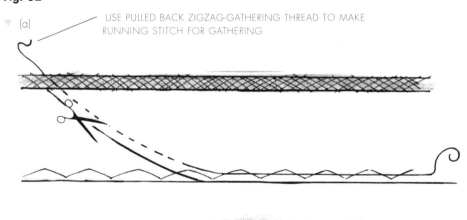

USE PULLED BACK ZIGZAG-GATHERING THREAD TO MAKE RUNNING STITCH FOR GATHERING

(a)

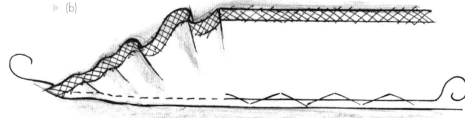

(b)

length of whatever is to be frilled. For example, for a curtain with a finished length of 2.5 m (98½ in) you will need 5m (196 in) of strip gathered back to 2.5 m (98½ in). Fine fabrics such as net can require up to four times the length. Heavy fabrics can take much less. You will therefore have to experiment.

Do not have vertical frilling too wide, especially if the fabric you are using is lightweight because frilling quickly responds to the force of gravity and droops towards the floor. A width of 8 cm (3 in) is about the maximum a frill can be unless it is to hang downwards (a gathered valance is a downward hanging frill if you think about it!).

When discussing styling with a client, decide whether the frilling is to be 'put-on' to a seam or 'put-in'. In the first method, the raw edge is enclosed within a seam and in the second a frill with no raw edges is machined, down

its face, on to the right side of the face fabric.

CONTRAST BINDING FOR FRILLING

This can be achieved on frilling in two ways.

METHOD 1

Cut the contrast to be 4 cm (1⅝ in) wide and join these strips. Cut the face fabric for both front and back to the required width plus seam allowances – 2 cm (¾ in) for the 'put-in' edge and 1 cm (⅜ in) for the edge to which the contrast binding is to be attached.

Right side to right side machine the contrast binding to the top edge of the first side of the face fabric strip at the 1 cm (⅜ in) mark. Repeat this for the second side of the face fabric strip, see Fig. 83 (a). Iron the resultant seams inwards and flat, then fold the contrast strip in half and iron it, see Fig. 83 (b).

Apply zigzag gathering to the raw edges.

METHOD 2

This is similar to applying piping with a cording foot. You will need 4 cm (1⅝ in) wide strips of contrast joined. Fold this round a length of piping cord and insert between the two layers of frilling strips. Machine in place, using a cording foot for preference, or a zip foot, for a distance of 40–50 cm (16–20 in), then stop. Leaving the machine needle in the fabric, lift the machine foot and pull the cord almost completely through the machined section. Lower the machine foot and repeat the process until you have completed the quantity of contrast-bound frilling that you require. Press thoroughly and carefully to ensure that the contrast binding is standing proud of the face fabric. This is a very quick and efficient method of making up contrast-bound frilling. It is a good method for making Type 2 frilling (page 103).

Fig. 83

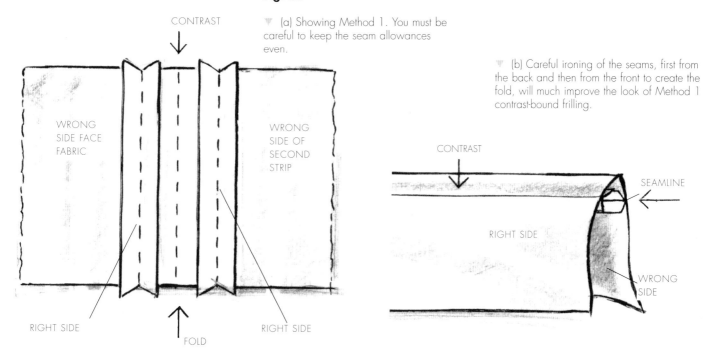

CONTRAST

(a) Showing Method 1. You must be careful to keep the seam allowances even.

(b) Careful ironing of the seams, first from the back and then from the front to create the fold, will much improve the look of Method 1 contrast-bound frilling.

WRONG SIDE FACE FABRIC

WRONG SIDE OF SECOND STRIP

RIGHT SIDE

RIGHT SIDE

FOLD

CONTRAST

SEAMLINE

RIGHT SIDE

WRONG SIDE

TYPES OF FRILLING

TYPE 1

A simple folded frill. The strips must be double the required finished width plus seam allowances. A finished width of 8 cm (3 in) requires strips 20 cm (8 in) wide. Join the strips right side to right side, trim and iron the seams. Cut off the lengths you need and fold each strip in half right side to right side. Machine across the ends to neaten, and then turn the ends out and press. Apply the zigzag gathering.

TYPE 2

Frilling with a single contrast-bound edge and two layers of fabrics. This type of frilling requires three separate strips of materials: a back, a front and the contrast binding. It is usually sufficient to cut the contrast binding 4 cm (1⅝ in) wide and the other two strips should be of the finished width plus 3 cm (1³⁄₁₆ in) of seam allowance each. It is more reliable, however, to overestimate the width of the second two strips slightly and then to cut back to the required width, plus seam allowances, after all the frilling has been made and before the zigzag gathering is applied. This type of frilling is very time-consuming to cut, make up and iron so be sure that you charge the client appropriately. See Figs. 84 (a), (b) and (c).

TYPE 3

A contrast-bound frill using only two layers of fabric. If the finished width of frill is 8 cm (3 in), cut face fabric strips at 10 cm (4 in). Cut contrast binding at 12.5 cm (5 in). Join, trim and iron the seams of all the strips. At the 1 cm (⅜ in) mark, right sides together, join the main fabric strip to the contrast strip. Open out and fold the contrast colour back over the seam, making sure that both the seam allowances face away from you. Trim the 1 cm (⅜ in) seam allowance to make sure that it is even – you can reduce it to 5 mm (³⁄₁₆ in) at this point if you want a delicate looking contrast binding – and fold the contrast back and under the wrong side of the face fabric. Iron carefully to make sure that the seam allowances face into the fold because all the layers of seam allowance will help to support the frill and to keep it looking crisp. Apply zigzag gathering. See Figs. 85 (a), (b) and (c).

▶ The position of the tie-backs can dramatically change the look of a simple curtain treatment. Easy access to French windows is needed.

TYPE 4

A double-bound contrast frill using two layers of fabrics. This construction is suitable for a 'put-on' frill. Cut the main fabric in strips to the required finished width. Cut the contrast colour strips 4 cm (1⅝ in) wider. Join the strips. Trim the seams and iron open. Right sides together, machine the two strips together at 1 cm (⅜ in). Pin the opposing side in place before machining to prevent the materials from travelling and dragging. Machine at 1 cm (⅜ in). See Figs. 86 (a), (b) and (c).

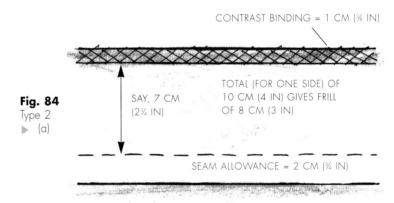

CONTRAST BINDING = 1 CM (⅜ IN)

Fig. 84
Type 2
▶ (a)

SAY, 7 CM (2¾ IN)

TOTAL (FOR ONE SIDE) OF 10 CM (4 IN) GIVES FRILL OF 8 CM (3 IN)

SEAM ALLOWANCE = 2 CM (¾ IN)

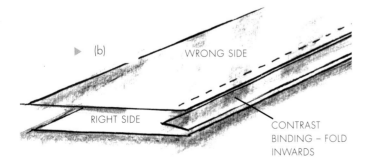

▶ (b)

WRONG SIDE

RIGHT SIDE

CONTRAST BINDING – FOLD INWARDS

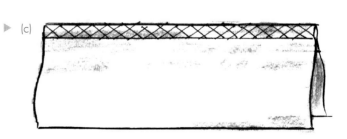

▶ (c)

Cut off the lengths you will need so that you can turn each length inside out separately . . . it is hardly possible to turn a really long length inside out in one go! Machine across one end of the cut lengths to make a strong point against which to push a yardstick to turn the tube inside out. Turn the tube inside out, cut off the machined end and let the yardstick drop through. Iron the tubes so that the seams lie flat and out towards the sides, and make sure that the contrast-bound edges are as even as possible.

With a Type 4 frill it is not possible to use zigzag gathering to gather it up because the gathering will have to be removed. Load the bobbin of your machine with strong thread, adjust the stitch length to very long and the tension to loose and make two lines of straight stitching about 2 cm (¾ in) apart down the middle and with the wrong side of the frill upwards so that, eventually, you can pull the strong bobbin thread out easily after you have attached the frill to the item. A put-on frill looks best with the gathering placed about one-third down its width if it is to be used horizontally and at the half-way mark if it is to be used vertically. Machine the frill in place down the middle of the two lines of stitching.

This type of frill has a number of decorative applications – i.e. for making rosettes.

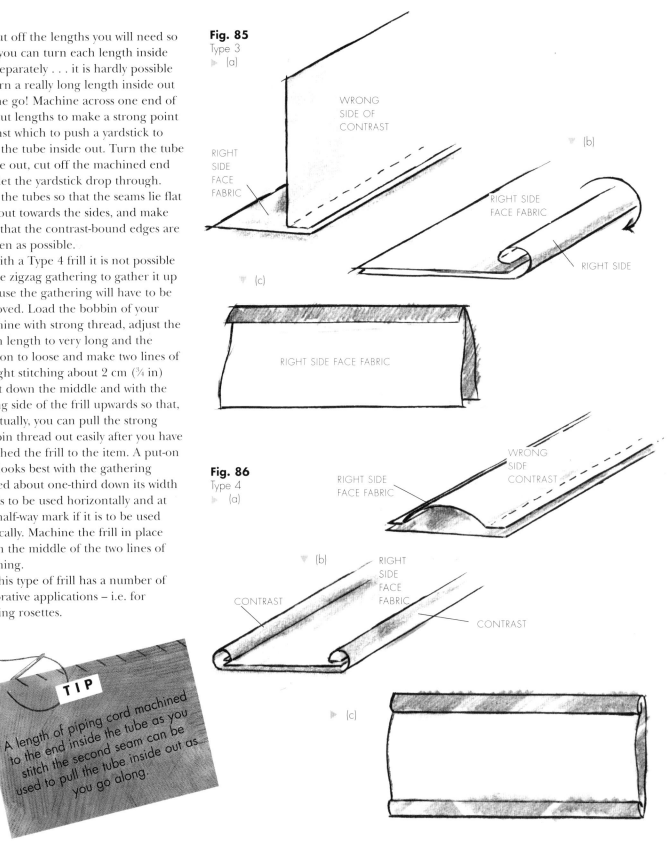

Fig. 85
Type 3
▶ (a)

WRONG SIDE OF CONTRAST

RIGHT SIDE FACE FABRIC

(b)

RIGHT SIDE FACE FABRIC

RIGHT SIDE

▼ (c)

RIGHT SIDE FACE FABRIC

WRONG SIDE CONTRAST

RIGHT SIDE FACE FABRIC

Fig. 86
Type 4
▶ (a)

▼ (b)

RIGHT SIDE FACE FABRIC

CONTRAST

CONTRAST

▶ (c)

TIP

A length of piping cord machined to the end inside the tube as you stitch the second seam can be used to pull the tube inside out as you go along.

— 104 —

TYPE 5

Double contrast bound put-on frill with lining or main fabric as backing. Cut strips of main fabric and lining (or main fabric backing strips) 2 cm (¾ in) narrower than the required finished width. Cut contrast strip 4 cm (1¾ in) wide and remember that you will need double the usual calculation because you have two sides of strip to contrast bind. Join, trim and iron all the seams of all the strips. Machine the first side of the three layers of fabrics as you would for a single contrast-bound edge (by using the cording foot and a length of piping cord). Pin the opposing side at 50 cm (20 in) intervals to prevent fabric drag and remove the pins as you machine the contrast-bound strip into place. Cut off the required lengths. Machine across one end and use a yardstick to push the tube inside out. Iron very carefully to ensure that the contrast binding stands proud and even from the main fabric. See Figs. 87 (a), (b) and (c).

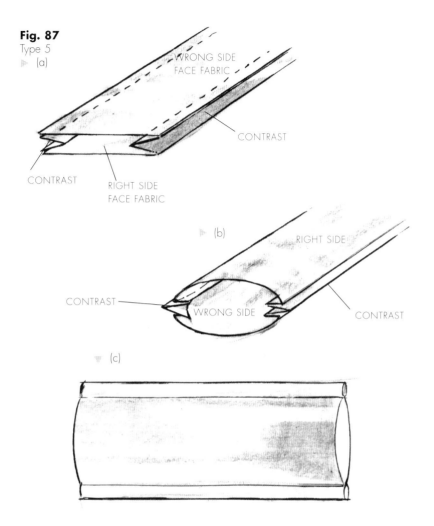

Fig. 87
Type 5
(a)

WRONG SIDE FACE FABRIC

CONTRAST

CONTRAST

RIGHT SIDE FACE FABRIC

(b)

RIGHT SIDE

CONTRAST

WRONG SIDE

CONTRAST

(c)

ROSETTES

A soft furnishing rosette does *not* look like the sort of thing which is pinned on to a horse at a gymkhana. Rosettes are great fun to make and you can indulge in exotic decorative techniques and combinations of materials. See the examples shown in Fig. 88.

The size of a rosette is determined by the position the rosette is to have. Pin up the pelmet or swags and experiment with circles of paper or bunched up scraps of material to decide what size you want the finished rosette to be.

Do not make rosettes at the start of a job because they are the final touch

and are created in relation to the overall size and styling of whatever it is that you have made.

I make rosettes on a base of two circles of buckram covered in face fabric. One circle is of hessian buckram and the other of fusible heading buckram, see Fig. 89 (a). The circles are usually about 8 cm (3 in) in diameter with the covering material cut bigger, though the size of these circles must be adjusted depending on the size of the rosette you envisage. The hessian buckram is dampened and the covering ironed on to the buckram centrally with the excess brought up

and round the back and also ironed into place. Cover the fusible buckram circle in the same way, minus the damping.

The choux are made of a circle of fabric three to four times wider than the base circles (it depends on how generous you want the crumpling to be) with zigzag gathering applied round the edge at the 1 cm (¾ in) mark, see Fig. 89 (b). Gather the circle up round a cylinder such as a cut-off from a fabric bolt cylinder. Knot off firmly, with the cylinder in place and then remove the cylinder, see Fig. 89 (c).

Flatten the 'shower cap' out so that the gathered centre is in the middle and the gathering is evenly disposed. Apply a generous coating of rubber-based adhesive carefully to the gathered raw edge of the 'shower cap' and then place the fusible buckram circle centrally over the glue wrong side up, see Fig. 89 (e). Press it down firmly and allow the glue to dry. Make up as many choux/rosettes as you are going to need to this stage.

When the glue is dry, thread a needle with strong thread and knot it. Crumple and twist the 'shower cap' to an attractive arrangement and secure it with stab stitches to hold the crumpling in place, see Fig. 89 (c).

For a choux rosette which is going to be suspended, say on a pelmet, you will now need to cut strips of face fabric about 25 cm (10 in) long and 10 cm (4 in) wide to make a tag. Fold the sides into the middle and iron the folds in place, see Fig. 89 (f). Folded over, this strip will make a tag which will suspend the rosette. Glue it to the back of the choux with the second, buckram, circle glued on top of it, see Fig. 89 (g). The tag is simply attached with a staple gun to the pelmet board to suspend the rosette at a suitable position.

Fig. 88

▲ (a) A simple choux.

▲ (b) Choux with a contrast-bound frill.

▲ (c) Maltese cross with a choux.

▲ (d) Whorl of contrast-bound frilling.

▲ (e) Choux with contrast-covered button.

▲ (f) Choux with contrast-bound pleats and a covered button.

Fig. 89

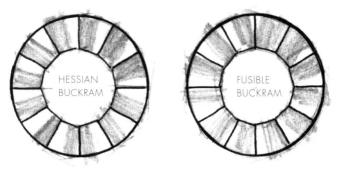

For a choux rosette which is going to be attached to, say, a tie-back, you will need to use really strong thread (preferably nylon or linen) to stab through the buckram circle from right side to wrong side and then from wrong side to right side at the points marked on Fig. 89 (h), leaving long tails which you can subsequently use to tie or sew the choux rosette in position.

(a) Two circles of buckram covered with face fabric.

RIGHT SIDE
SIZE: ABOUT FOUR TIMES
THAT OF SMALL CIRCLES

(b) Large circle of contrast or face fabric with zigzag-gathering round outer edge.

(c) Large circle of fabric pulled up resembling a shower cap!

(d) Large circle flattened out and glued to fusible buckram circle.

Fig. 89 (continued)

◀ (e) Twist, primp and stab stitch the large circle on to the fusible buckram circle to achieve the crumpled look.

▲ (f) Tag of folded face fabric about 15 cm (6 in) long finished length.

▼ (h) If the choux is for a tie-back, or needs to be sewn in place, put long, strong threads through wrong side of buckram circle and use them to attach the choux.

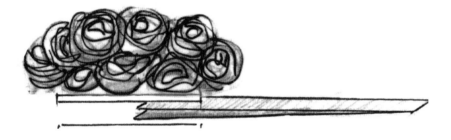

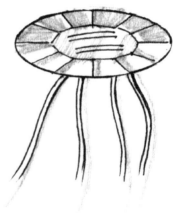

▲ (g) Glue the folded tag to the hessian buckram circle, then glue the choux on its fusible buckram circle to the hessian buckram. Clip together round the edges to ensure that the glue holds well.

MAKING A MALTESE CROSS WITH A CHOUX CENTRE

For a Maltese cross with a choux centre, use Type 4 frilling (page 104) to make the four 'arms'. These arms are made of the frilling strip which is cut for folding to a suitable length to make the required size of arm. You will have to experiment to decide the best size but do not have the arms too long or they will look much more like a windmill than a rosette.

Place these folded strips side by side and feed them through the sewing machine in one operation to apply zigzag gathering at the raw edges. Pull up and knot off the zigzag gathering.

Dispose the gathering so that the arms are equidistant. Apply a good amount of glue to the back of the arms just over the gathered area and then apply the right side of the fusible buckram circle to the back of the arms. When the glue for the arms has dried, the choux centre can be applied in the same way as described on page 107, with the suspension being either of the two methods, depending on eventual usage.

BOWS

In soft furnishing bows should be made up in separate sections to achieve a crisp, tailored, well constructed look. If you want an informal effect, knot a tubular length of fabric into a bow.

The size of the bow must be determined by experimenting to get one which looks proportionately right. An over-long bow section will droop. Make the width of both the bow and the loop generous so that there is plenty of texture from the folds.

A formal bow is made in three sections, using a tube of material made to the appropriate width to achieve the desired affect and cutting off each section separately to make them up.

Make a long tube of material to the required finished width. Turn it out and iron it so that the seam is to the centre back. Cut off a length which, when doubled on itself (plus seam allowances), will be long enough to form the bow section. Form this strip into a circle by placing right sides together and making a seam, see Fig. 90 (a). Place the seam to the centre back and use the seamline as a guide for sewing a line of zigzag-gathering stitches which you will use to gather up the fabric to make the folds of the bow.

Fig. 90

◁ (a) The bow section. Join the ends at the back, then zigzag-gather down the centre and pull up.

MAKE KNOT/LOOP IN SAME WAY. GATHER UP ALONG BACK SEAM ONLY

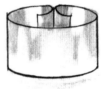

ZIGZAG-GATHER ALL LAYERS DOWN CENTRE AND PULL UP

▷ (b) The knot or loop section. Make this in the same way as the bow section but smaller.

CUT ENDS STRAIGHT OR DIAGONALLY. TURN IN AND SLIP-STITCH

▲ (c) The tails section.

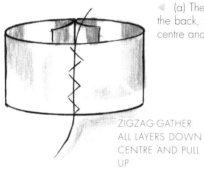

◁ (d) The bow section is slipped through the knot section and the tails are pulled through behind the bow. Arrange the bow attractively and sew the component parts together so that they do not slip. Sew or use Velcro to attach, or sew on a small brass ring if the bow is to be used above a picture.

Make the knot or loop section in the same way but on a smaller scale, see Fig. 90 (b). Experiment to achieve a pleasing length for the tail section, see Fig. 90 (c). Fold the tube in at the ends and slip-stitch the fold to neaten. The ends can be cut on the straight or on the diagonal. Slip the tail section through the loop and to the back of the bow and stitch it in place, see Fig. 90 (d).

The bow can be made to hold its shape by padding it out, between the two layers, with a little twist of polyester wadding.

A very elegant bow can be made following the diagrams in Fig. 91 again you will have to experiment to achieve the right size for the effect you want. The bow section is made from two layers of fabric leaving a short, unmachined section, near the knot, so that it can be turned inside out.

Fig. 91

▶ (a) Two half circles machined together and then turned inside out.

MACHINE FROM HERE

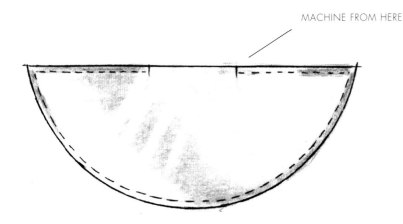

▶ (b) Bring both points A to meet at point B and sew together. Zigzag-gather or hand-gather the front and pull up. Construct the bow in the same way as before.

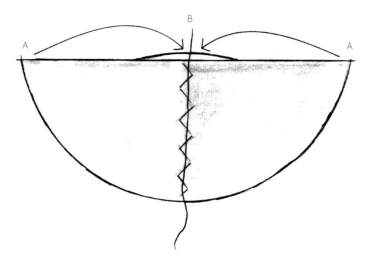

8

SWAGS AND
TAILS

Making swags and tails is one of the most creative aspects of soft furnishing. However, swags and tails are really only suitable for use in rooms with high ceilings and large windows. For the maker of soft furnishings, it is a profitable skill which looks difficult and complicated to the 'outsider' but which is really only an extension of straightforward curtain-making. All the basic tailoring methods used in making curtains are used to make swags and tails . . . it is the cutting for the styling that is the relatively tricky part.

Bear in mind that what you are creating is a form of sculpture. Shadows and depth are given to the fabric by draping and folding so this is a treatment which looks particularly good in a plain, light coloured material.

These simple swags have been backed with a ruched hard pelmet in a strong contrasting colour, which is also used in the tails.

The styling must be compatible with the fabric, the room and its contents. You are aiming for pleasing proportions, well formed and even draping, and a certain 'magic' quality.

Swags and tails, with all the other things such as jabots, trumpets, space fillers and rosettes, are made as separate pieces and suspended from a pelmet board in the correct order to achieve the end result. Space fillers will go up first in the correct position, then the swags, then the tails, then, perhaps, draped rope and, finally the trumpets and rosettes.

POINTS TO CONSIDER

There are certain points to consider before you start draping and cutting the fabric.

Although it is often recommended, it is not always possible to cut swags on the bias because the fabric you are using will dictate whether you cut on

the straight or on the cross. Stripes, for instance, (and an emphatic moiré counts as a stripe) cannot be cut on the cross for a swag because the result, when draped up, is a mess. In tails, too, stripes remain 'flat' looking if the tail is cut for simple vertical folding; it is better to think about a curved, steeple shaping or gathering the heading rather than folding it.

Patterned fabrics must be cut to continue the illusion that the pattern is lined up with the curtains underneath. Some thought must also be given to the placement of a motif which can be repeated in the same place on every swag and every tail at each window. It may not be possible to use the same motif on each side of the window because the fabric pattern may not allow it. Just make sure that every item at each window matches its partners at all the other windows in the room, see Fig. 92.

If it is planned for the tails to be a simple diagonal cut with simple, vertical folds, you must test the material for its folding characteristics, in the position you plan for the cutting of the tails, to see what happens when you fold, first, from right to left and then from left to right. It may be that on one side one part of the pattern will block together in a dominant way, and on the other it will look quite different. You may have to modify the template placement to rectify this, or think about gathering the heading.

Swags must look as if they are draped from end to end of the pelmet board in a 'natural' way. But all the items must be long enough, and so shaped, that they cover the tops of the windows and the headings of the curtains. It is preferable for swags to have an uneven number of 'pleats' and tails to have an uneven number of folds. See Fig. 93.

Fig. 92

▷ Make sure that the chosen anchoring motif is the same on all the swags and tails at all the windows.

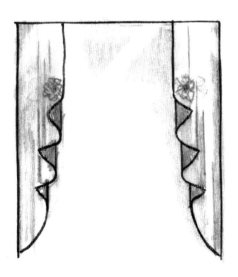

Fig. 93

The swags and tails shown in (a) look wrong. The tails are too wide and the swag does not give the illusion of continuing to the end of the pelmet board. Those shown in (b), (c) and (d) give the right impression. The tails shown in (e) widen towards the base from a narrow heading. This treatment is elegant and feminine.

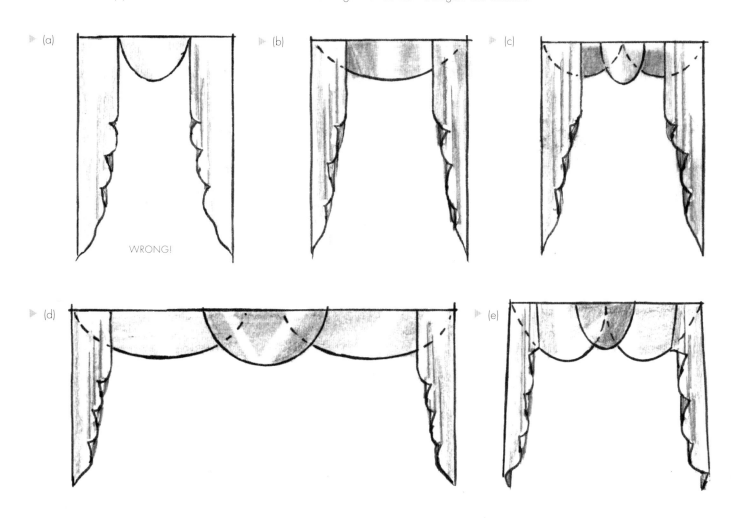

DRAPING SWAGS AND TAILS

For draping swags and tails it is absolutely essential to have a draping board (page 114). It should be made of the sort of soft fibreboard into which pins can be stuck easily. Ideally, one whole wall of your workroom should be covered in soft fibreboard, placed with its top high enough to accommodate the draping of tails which are usually between 2 m (78¾ in) and 2.5 m (98½ in) long.

On the board mark a straight line at a height which is comfortable for you to reach – if you are very short, you may have to step up on to a box. If possible, have this horizontal line at least 3.5 m (140 in) long and 'reinforce' it with 2 cm (¾ in) masking tape applied along its length, above and on the line; this masking tape acts as a seam allowance measurement.

From the middle of the line,

downwards, mark a vertical line and do the same at several other equidistant points along the length, reinforcing these lines with masking tape. Mark off the tape, both vertically and horizontally, with a felt-tip pen to show 5cm (2 in) and 10 cm (4 in) measurements – the vertical measuring off should start at the base of the horizontal tape, see Fig. 94. As you will frequently need to rig up treatments on this board to check them for proportions and drape, it is worth having a big board and marking the tape with all the measurements used often.

HOW TO DRAPE A SWAG

You will need a good supply of long, strong pins and a 6–8 m (6½–8¾ yd) length of link brass chain. Stab plenty of the pins into the draping board above the horizontal line ready for use.

The styling and measurements will have already been decided.

To work out the width for the heading of a swag which is not going to overlap another one, divide the length of the pelmet board by the intended number of swags, but in order to lessen the bulk at the outside corners, reduce

the length of the pelmet board by 10cm (4 in) and divide the result by the number of swags.

With the heading width of the swag calculated, mark it off on the horizontal line on the draping board with pins. The measurement should be centralized over a vertical line.

Hook a free end of the chain on to one of the pins and then loop the chain carefully on to the other pin so that the curve measures the proposed drop of the swag – this gives a natural curve. If you are uncertain about the finished look of the proposed swags, it is a good idea to rig the chain so that it creates a series of loops. By doing this, you may discover that you need fillers between the curves of each swag to hide the top of the window, or that you

need to amend the design so that the swags overlap to a point deep enough to cover the top of the curtain headings and the top of the window. The narrower a swag is at its heading, the deeper and closer together will be the curves of all the swags. You may need three swags, rather than two, to solve the problem of covering the top of the window. When you are satisfied that you have solved all these questions, you can loop the chain to get the necessary shape to make one swag to the measurements you have decided.

To make a template for the swag, you will need a piece of lining material (for lined-only) or interlining (for interlined) at least twice the depth of the swag and 50 cm (20 in) wider. I pull fabric for swag templates straight

Fig. 94

▼ Sheets of soft fibreboard are screwed to the workroom wall with strips of masking tape marked to show 5 cm (2 in) and 10 cm (4 in) measurements.

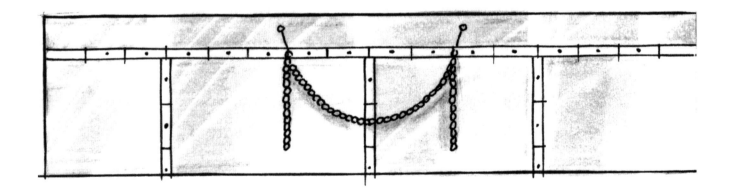

from the bolt and use the result in one of the swags – this way there is minimum wastage. You will find that it is necessary to make a new template for every job because the material and the dimensions will be different each time.

Pull off enough draping material to give yourself plenty to work with down the length. Pencil a straight line about 1.5–2 m (60–75 in) long down the middle of the length and make sure that the top of the material is cut to be straight. To make the template, you will drape on the straight (though you may use the template on the bias), using the pencilled line to keep the material folding on the straight and into its 'pleats'. You must be prepared to make endless adjustments to get the draping right. Developing a technique and lifting and folding which you can do easily and well can be a prolonged and exhausting process.

With the vertical pencilled line to the middle mark of the pinned marks for the swag measurements, pin the top of the material on line and to the top of the horizontal line of masking tape, see Fig. 95 (a).

The side of the swag to which you work your draping will depend upon whether you are left- or right-handed, but the side does not matter. Depending on the depth and the shape of the swag, you will normally be working three to seven pleats into the drape. You will be working to create a 'fan' across the upper corner of the swag, starting about a third of the way into the half-way measurement. Strangely, the first pleat is usually quite deep on fabric and shallow on pleating. Pin in place. Pin the material on the other side up with a pin, roughly, so that the pleat is held in place and the vertical pencilled line remains hanging down straight, see Fig. 95 (b).

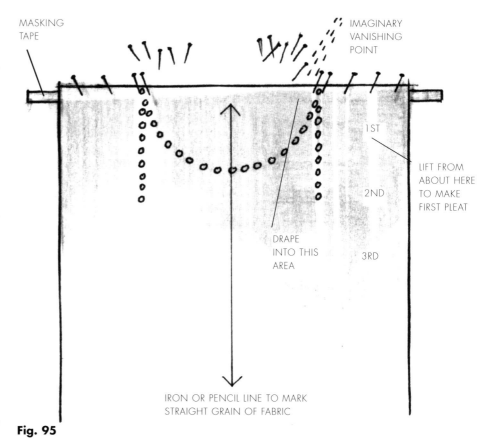

Fig. 95

▲ (a) Make sure that you have plenty of strong pins stuck into the board before you start draping. Drape into an imaginary 'vanishing point' about 30 cm (12 in) above the horizontal line.

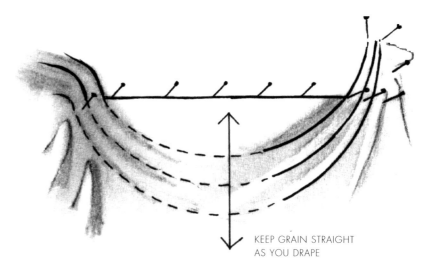

▲ (b) Use the side of your left hand, held at the required angle, to pull the first pleat up against the board while your right hand lifts and tucks the pleat. Work in reverse if you are left-handed. This is very difficult to start with, but like riding a bicycle, the 'trick' is suddenly achieved.

Continue lifting and 'fanning' the material, constantly making sure that the pencilled vertical line remains straight, until your last pleat has its base on line with the chain, which you can feel through the fabric.

Stand back to examine how well you have done the draping . . . the fanning should look even and natural and the spaces between the pleats should grade, slightly, from top to bottom. When seen from the side, by squinting at it, the swag should also look even and 'graded', see Fig. 96 (a).

When the draping satisfies you, from all directions, cut away the excess fabric, using the chain as a guide, on the draped side. First, feel for the chain and use a felt-tip pen (contrary to workroom 'rules'!) to mark the fabric with the line the chain indicates. Take this marking up and beyond the

Fig. 96

▷ (a) Seen from the side, the swag should look like this.

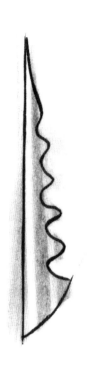

▷ (b) The swag should not look like this.

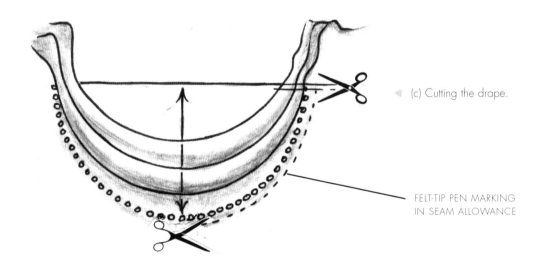

◁ (c) Cutting the drape.

FELT-TIP PEN MARKING IN SEAM ALLOWANCE

▷ (d) The template will look similar to one of the diagrams.

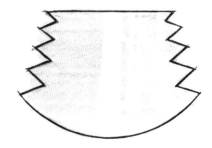

top line of the swag (move pins out of the way if necessary) and, using a ruler, mark a horizontal line with the top line of the masking tape as a guide. Mark a second line below the first 'chain' line to give you a 2 cm (¾ in) seam allowance.

Snip a hole on the seam allowance line at the halfway mark, which is the original vertical pencil line, and cut upwards on the seam allowance line to beyond the area of fanning, and then across on the horizontal line, see Fig. 96 (c). This may be difficult because there are many layers of material.

Remove all the pins and take the cut material down from the board. Use the vertical pencil line as a guide to fold the fabric down its length so that you can cut out the opposite side of the template to match the side you have draped. You will end up with a shape looking rather like a Christmas tree, see Fig. 96 (d).

MAKING SWAGS

With swags which are the shape shown in Fig. 97 (a) you have to drape first up to point A with the pleat being taken down to a point between B and C, and so on until you achieve the look you want.

With swags on the quarter shape shown in Figs. 97 (b) and (c) the template will have to be reversed when it is placed on the main fabric so that the pattern of the fabric faces the right way.

Check the drape of the completely cut swag template by re-draping it on the draping board. It should go back perfectly if you start at the top by pinching the first 'valley' together and then lining the pinched 'V' up so that its raw edges can be brought up and pinned to the top horizontal line. The usual rule is 'pinch the valleys forward and upwards and pull the peaks outwards'. Adjust and re-cut and trim if and where you feel it is necessary. The template is ready when you are satisfied with its shape and drape.

If you find that the swag template is too wide to fit the chosen face fabric, you will have to pattern-match and join the fabric in the area which requires extra width. These joins will hardly show.

Have the main fabric right side up on the table and choose the motif in the pattern which is going to be your 'anchor'. Place the template on the material so that it is either on the straight or on a true bias depending upon the type of fabric. Cut out the main fabric using the template as the pattern. Once you have cut one swag from the main fabric, you can use it to cut all the others, thus ensuring correct pattern placement.

When you have cut all the main fabric pieces required (which will include the pieces for the tails), smooth the lining on to the table wrong side up. If the main fabric is patterned, you will find that you use a lot less interlining and lining. Smooth interlining on top of the lining. Place

the main fabric swag shapes on the lining and interlining right side up and in such a way as to minimize fabric wastage. Remember that if the swags have been cut on the straight, the linings must also be cut on the straight; if the swags are cut on the bias, the linings must also be on the bias. Cut the linings out around the template – single pin the three layers together so that they do not become separated.

Interlock the face fabric section to the interlining according to the lines marked in Fig. 97 (d). Interlocking for swags needs to be much closer together and with a much tighter stitch than that which is used for curtains – this is because the layers must be well held together when re-draping. Do not take the interlocking too close to the points of the swag because the interlining is going to be cut back in this area. Start and finish the interlocking well within the seam allowances.

Fig. 97

▶ (a)

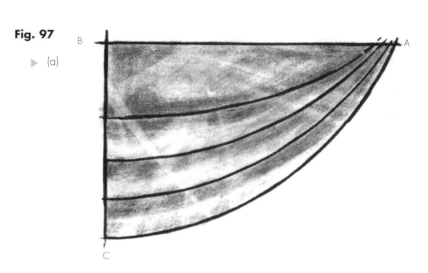

▼ (b)

▼ (c)

PLAIN FABRIC – RIGHT SIDE

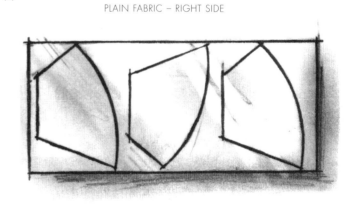

◀ These classic overlapping swags and tails are
a simple styling that does not demand much
experience in making soft furnishings.

When the interlocking is completed, cut away the interlining at 3 cm (1⅙ in) along the top horizontal and into and out of the points at the sides. Do not cut away the interlining on the base line. A careful long and short tacking stitch is sufficient to hold the interlining in place along this cut-back line, see Fig. 97 (e).

Pin the lining right side to right side of the interlined face fabric. Machine along the baseline, which is the hem of the swag. A very neat edge can be achieved by self- or contrast-piping this hem, in an all-in-one operation, if you machine the layers together using the cording foot. Cut away the excess interlining as close to the machine stitching as you can safely manage and

then trim the seam allowance back to 1 cm (⅜ in), notching if necessary to ensure a good drape.

'Put-on' trimmings, such as fringe, can be applied to the front of the swag, using the seam as a placement guide. To do this, open the swag out like a book, right side up. If you have a cording foot which is sufficiently large, it can often be used to attach fringe. Use strong, matching thread and a long stitch. The ends of fringe can be neatened by cutting off the twists which overlap into the top line seam allowance and then catching the ends into the casing which is used to finish and suspend the swag.

It is best, at this point, to make up one swag completely and to use it as

the model for all the others. This means that you must now turn it out and iron it. To interlock the lining, make the baseline of the swag face you with the lining uppermost and draw the lining forward and down until the sides of the swag begin to pull in and the inside of the lining has a rolled fold about 10 cm (4 in) above the baseline. Interlock the lining to the interlining along this fold and then space lines of interlocking roughly every 15 cm (6 in) above this to hold the lining firmly in place. The interlock stitching must be closer and tighter than that for curtains.

Swags (and tails) are headed or finished with a casing made of strips of lining material cut to a width of 15 cm

Fig. 97 (continued)

▼ (d) Interlocking on swags has to be smaller and tighter than that used for curtains. 'Fan' the interlocking out across the swag as shown.

▼ (e) Make sure that the long and short tacking stitches do not show on the right side too much! Most of this stitching will be hidden in the folds of the pleats.

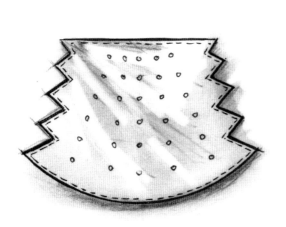

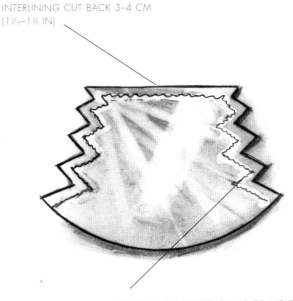

INTERLINING CUT BACK 3–4 CM (1⅙–1⅜ IN)

LONG AND SHORT TACKING TO HOLD INTERLINING IN POSITION

(6 in). Mark the strip with the correct measurement for the finished width of the swag and also with a middle point. Add generous turning allowances at the ends. Pin this strip to the draping board right side up and along the horizontal line. Re-drape the swag, raw edge to raw edge, on to the casing strip, casing the draping into the measured length and making sure that the re-drape is perfect. Use masking tape to hold the draping and pin the swag to the casing to hold the 'fan' in place, see Fig. 97 (f). Take it all to the machine for stitching.

Machine stitching a swag to its casing can be exceptionally hard because of the numerous layers of fabric. Sometimes it is not possible and the casing will have to be stitched in place by hand with the 'fan' cobbled to hold it, with the cobbling hidden under the casing. If the machine can cope with all the layers, you are lucky. Sew the casing to the back of the swag and then iron it up and forward. Finger-press a 2 cm (¾ in) seam allowance under, fold the ends in neatly and then machine along the fold from the front to enclose the raw edge. See Fig. 97 (g).

Swags are suspended from the pelmet board by the casing, using a staple gun.

▶ (f) Check the swag for length at the same time as you re-drape it on to a band of lining material. Hold the pleats in place with masking tape.

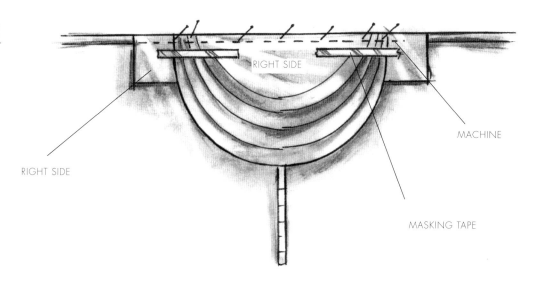

RIGHT SIDE

RIGHT SIDE

MACHINE

MASKING TAPE

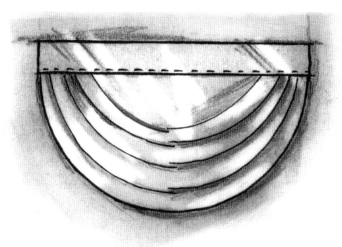

◀ (g) The finished swag, with the ends of the casing tucked in and the raw edge folded under and machined.

TAILS

Tails are simpler to make than swags but the template still needs careful draping and cutting. The templates for swags can be kept and re-used many times. Make them up in shortish, medium and long lengths, and adjust them for length as and where you need to.

The two basic styles for tails and the underlying shapes needed to achieve them are shown in Fig. 98. A single width of 140 cm (55⅛ in) wide fabric is generally sufficient unless the return is unusually wide.

TAIL: STYLE A

To achieve a template for a tail such as style A, use interlining cut to the shape and proportions outlined below. The line C–D can be cut straight or tapered according to personal preference.

The length of a tail is from the front corner of the return of the pelmet board down to a point at which you think it will look attractive in relation to the planned styling. Tails look much better cut on the long side rather than short. The leading edge of a tail – line A–B – should be cut to the same length as the swags at the point where the tails overlap the swag. This is not, however, a hard and fast rule.

Tails are not attractive if they are too wide from side to side. Three to five folds are sufficient; the latter will need a greater length to look proportionately right. Tails which have too precise a measurement between each fold look regimented and flat. It seems to look better if each fold is graded so that the resulting triangles of contrast lining are different in size. The biggest triangle should be at the bottom, then a smaller one and so on.

If you are using a patterned face fabric as the contrast in the tails rather than a plain fabric – or plain material as main fabric and patterned for contrast – you must be as careful to get the pattern placement in the same place in each tail as you would if you were using patterned material as the main fabric.

To make the template, cut a shape of interlining roughly to the shape and measurements shown in the diagrams for Style A. Pin this shape to the draping board with the return section pinned flat. Use another pin to hold the top of the leading edge in place about 20 cm (8 in) on from the end of the return section. Fold the material into folds within this area adjusting and moving the folds to fit. Stand back to see what sort of pleats and triangles have been produced. If the folding is satisfactory, you must mark it into place with a series of notches and snips at the top so that you can repeat the folding accurately on all the tails you make. This marking is similar to that found on dress patterns.

Templates for tails are reversible so you do not need to make separate

▷ Here the simplest of hard pelmets has been given drama by the addition of 'balloon tails'. These are bags of material gathered up on to an internal rope.

templates for the right-hand and left-hand sides.

Cut the leading edge of the template to a slight angle between A and B. This slight angle makes a tremendous difference to the look of straight-cut tails, lifting them from pedestrian to stylish.

Piping, frilling, fringe and so on give emphasis to the shape of a tail.

Tails are made up in the same way as a swag with interlining interlocked in place and the contrast backing machined in place along the baseline but not up the sides. Machine stitching the baseline makes for a much neater and crisper finish than slip-stitching by hand. Do not take the machining right to the ends of the baseline of the tail. Stop at the turning allowance points and reverse to reinforce. Cut away the excess interlining along the machine line of stitches, and on the diagonal at the turning allowance point to get excess fabric out of the way when you turn the turning allowance back and in.

Weight should be sewn on to the interlining at points B and D. Interlock the contrast lining into place, on the diagonal, using the baseline as your guide. Three diagonal lines of interlocking, quite close together, are sufficient. Serge stitch (page 45) the

Fig. 98

▷ Style A

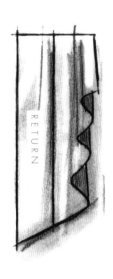
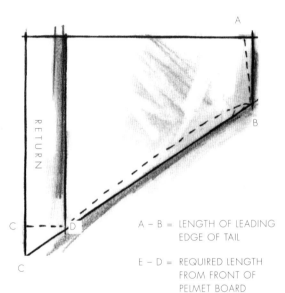
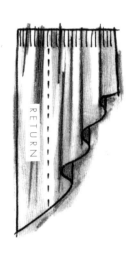

A – B = LENGTH OF LEADING
EDGE OF TAIL

E – D = REQUIRED LENGTH
FROM FRONT OF
PELMET BOARD
DOWNWARDS

▷ Style B

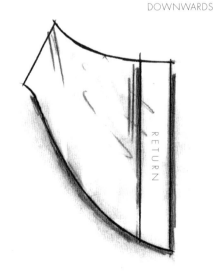

turning allowances in place as you would the edge of a curtain, folding the points at the base in neatly. Bring the lining over and slip-stitch it on line with the folded edge of the turning. Make sure that the point is neatly folded and sewn in place.

Remember that a long and heavy fringe will encroach on your contrast triangles, and you may have to re-drape in order to ensure that enough contrast is on display.

Also remember that tails, like Quarter Swags, must be reversed in the cutting out.

TAIL: STYLE B

It is the curved top line of Style B which makes the tail fall in folds which have a steeple-like shape. The first fold, nearest the return, is usually very small and the others are piled up much more on one another to achieve a top

which is narrowed in relation to the bottom. Each triangle should be graded in size. The base of the leading edge can be extended and cut to various curves to create a flute-like look if required.

Mark the folds with snips and notches so that you can repeat the same folds on each tail.

If the steeple tail has a sharply pointed end to the leading edge, machine the baseline *within* the turning allowances so that you can trim the interlining away and turn the turning allowances in, following the same sewing methods as for the side turning of a Style A tail.

FABRIC ESTIMATING FOR SWAGS AND TAILS

It is impossible to make up fabric estimates for swags and tails without knowing the width and pattern repeat

of the face fabric. It is best to make rough templates rather than risk quoting for too much or too little fabric. Swags and tails are very extravagant of material if it is patterned, especially if the pattern repeat is large. With a plain fabric you can sometimes use the tail templates in a top-to-toe arrangement which saves a great deal of material but you must first have seen the fabric in a largish piece to be able to decide about this (remember that plain materials are often woven so that there is an 'up' and a 'down' to the weave).

With patterned fabric, it is best to assume that you will need the full length of the swag or tail plus one pattern repeat per item. With plain fabric, you will need the full length of each item plus a bit extra.

Remember that you will probably have copious offcuts to make frilling,

9

PACKING AND HANGING CURTAINS

Much of this advice is equally applicable when you are moving house as when you are preparing to hang curtains for a client.

Get a supply of rolls of tubular plastic in two sizes: one about 40–50 cm (16–20 in) wide and the second about 1m (yd) wide. Plastic tubing for packing is available from some of the wholesale suppliers. Everything should be packed in plastic because the weather might change from good to bad while you are travelling, and you should not risk rain damaging the contents.

Tape-headed curtains should be packed flat, folded sides to middle down their length with the lining to the outside, see Fig. 99. They can be pulled up to size on site. It is, of course, possible to pull the curtains up to size in the workroom (add a small

charge for this service) but the decision as to whether to do this will rather depend upon how long the curtains are going to be stored before they are hung.

Hand-headed curtains need very careful folding and it is much easier to do this with two people. Fold them in such a way that the pleats will be in the correct position when the curtain is hanging.

All types of curtains should be tied with offcuts at intervals down their

length to prevent the careful folding from falling apart. Ease them into a suitable length of tubular plastic and seal each end with an offcut tie so that the package looks like a huge cracker. This will enable you to keep the tubing to use again.

Mark each package with its contents and the room for which it is intended.

Try to transport the curtains without folding the packages across their width to avoid any unnecessary creasing.

Fig. 99

▲ Curtains are folded sides to middle with the lining outermost. Use offcuts to tie them down their length.

ADVANCE PREPARATIONS

Hanging can present unforeseen difficulties. On one occasion I was to hang a simple Roman blind and had anticipated it would be fairly difficult because the top of the window was behind a landing on the stairs. I thought that, with the window opened,

I should just be able to manage. When I returned to do the job, the decorators had painted the window firmly shut! My head would only just fit in the tiny space between the landing and the window, and the job became a dangerous nightmare.

On another job the client lowered the ceiling without telling me. The result was that the pelmet board was so close to the new ceiling that I had no room to wield a staple gun to fix the swags and tails. The pelmet boards had to be taken off the walls so that the swags and tails

▶ The source for this unusual window treatment can be traced to the end of the eighteenth century when coat pegs were used to suspend muslins above windows to soften the outline.

could be attached, which made it extremely heavy to lift back. Luckily I had help, but the job took hours longer than anticipated.

Untrained people who have the temerity to call themselves 'interior decorators' can also pull tricks like this and you have every right to be put out. If *their* activities cause you to have to make alterations and extra journeys, you are entitled to charge for these, but tell them that you intend to do so.

Hanging curtains is *dangerous* work. As soon as possible you should arrange insurance to cover yourself against accident and damage to your client's property while it is in your possession, in transit or on site while hanging. You will also need to insure against damage to the property of clients in their homes – it is frighteningly easy to knock over a valuable vase. Sometimes you will have to take out over-ride insurance to cover the replacement cost of very valuable goods, such as passmenterie.

Wear sensible clothes for climbing up and down ladders and be sure your shoes have non-slip soles.

There are times when hanging can be difficult and complicated and you will have to use common sense and imagination to overcome problems. This is why it is sensible to take everything you might possibly need with you when hanging curtains in a client's house. The length of the list opposite may dismay you but you will be able to cope with unexpected problems more calmly. A professional track fitter should really top the list! Keep the tools separate from the household tools. Check and update supplies frequently because it is very frustrating to be doing a job and to find a necessary item is missing.

On arriving at the client's house, make sure that the space in front of the windows is completely cleared of furniture, pictures, lamps and ornaments. Thoughtful clients will have already done this for you! Choose a space for the discarded packaging and also lay a dust-sheet on the floor to use as an 'island' on which to keep all your equipment, which will help to prevent loss. Position the ladders for safety and convenience, with one at each side of the window so that you do not have to move a ladder from side to side continually.

With a properly organized job the new pelmet boards and tracks will, of course, have been installed already or you will be using the originals. If the tracks are old, it may be necessary to take them down to wash them free of dirt and dust because a good clean will make them work better. Use silicone spray (available from wholesalers) to lubricate the gliders. On a big job it is likely that a professional track fitter will be involved and you should ask that he deals with any necessary cleaning and lubricating beforehand.

Test the pelmet board, track or pole for firmness of fixing before you begin hanging the curtains.

Fig. 100

▼ Drills for masonry have a top shaped like a little house (a) and drills for wood have a scoop-like top (b).

▷ (a)   ▷ (b)

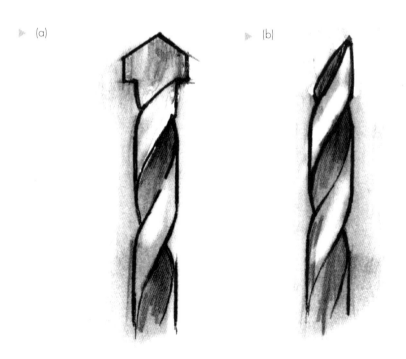

EQUIPMENT FOR HANGING

- An estate car with a roof rack

- Your work apron

- Two lightweight folding ladders with a platform top and a reliable method of staying fixed. About 1.50 m (60 in) from platform to floor. The feet should have rubber caps to prevent damage to floors and carpets. Hire extra long ladders if the job requires it. Transport the ladders on the roof rack

- An electric drill with a variety of wood and masonry bits. Tie the key to the handle if necessary

- A brush steamer and a pair of rubber gloves to protect your hands from the steam (or a professional steamer when you can afford one)

- An electric extension cord (if it is the wind-up kind, it must be used with the flex fully extended to prevent heat build-up turning to fire)

- An electric adaptor plug

- A portable vacuum cleaner, dustpan and brush, rags and washing up liquid

- A dust-sheet

- Specialist silicone lubricating spray to 'oil' the tracks

- A simple pack of primary first-aid equipment

- Picnic food and drink. Reading material (you need a rest at some point!)

- A compartmentalized carrying case to hold screws, nails and so on

- A small pot of Vaseline to lubricate screws and to help prevent them from rusting

- Plenty of assorted steel screws of varying lengths and thicknesses, both slot-head and cross-head

- Plenty of assorted brass screws of varying lengths and thicknesses, both round and flat-head

- A supply of assorted nails for wood and masonry

- A supply of brass tie-back hooks

- A staple gun and boxes of different length staples

- Rings – hollow brass and plastic, small and large

- Bulk supplies of curtain hooks in metal and plastic and compatible with the make of heading tape you have used.

- Bulk supply of metal pin hooks

- Chromed eyelet screws for hanging blinds

- Long shank eyelet screws for hanging curtains round returns

- A large supply of brass panel pins 1.5–2 cm (⅝–¾ in) long

- A supply of copper hardboard nails 1.5–2 cm (⅝–¾ in) long

- A reel of nylon cord for blinds

- Some 'acorns' in wood and plastic to tidy cord ends

- Scissors, needles, pins, a plait of multi-coloured threads and a seam ripper

- A hand drill

- A tack lifter

- A bradawl – impale the point in a cork for safety

- A selection of plastic plugs for plugging holes in walls to reinforce screws (you will need a wide variety to cope with contingencies)

- Screwdrivers (buy a box containing a pistol-handled screwdriver with a selection of interchangeable heads – very useful). One long screwdriver, and one stubby

- Hacksaw and blades for metal and wood. A panel saw

- Sheets of sandpaper

- Pincers and pliers

- Heavy claw hammer and lightweight pin hammer

- Expanding steel tape measure

- A spirit level

- A ready-cut bag of clear plastic strip to dress/tie the curtains

- Velcro stick-on spots. Drawing pins.

- A camera, flash and film (ask the client's permission before taking photographs)

- A portable sewing machine (just in case!)

HANGING THE CURTAINS

On a straightforward job the curtains are hung first. Pull them up to size so that the cords are to the window edge of the curtain. Tie the cords, firmly, and either tuck the tails into a ready-made pocket or form them into a hank and poke the hank under the 'bridge' cords in the heading tape. Cords can easily get tangled with the pulley mechanism so you should make sure that they are well, and firmly, stored.

Use hooks which are compatible with the type of heading tape you have used. Be sure to use metal hooks if the gliders are made of metal and plastic hooks if the gliders are made of plastic. The hooks should be inserted at intervals of, roughly, every sixth pocket. Adjustments may have to be made to the positioning for length, which is why a multi-pocket tape is so good. Insert hooks to match the holes of the crossover arm as this will help to carry the weight at the most vulnerable part of the track. Do the same careful spacing at the window edge to make sure that the curtain hooks line up with the return hook and the holes which are usually found in the fixings at the end of the track.

Curtains with handmade headings are suspended with pin hooks (or brass hooks sewn on by hand). If the track is one of the standard makes, the point for insertion of the pin is 7.5 cm (3 in) below the heading line, and the hook must always be placed just to one side of the stitching line, rather than through it, for strength. Make sure that the pin points do not show through at the front.

Distribute the gliders within one third of the track to both the left and the right of the window. Heave the weight of the curtain over your shoulder in such a way that you can carry it up the ladder and present the heading to the gliders and crossover arm as quickly as possible. Start by hooking a window edge curtain hook to the return hook, a leading edge curtain hook to the crossover arm, and a middle curtain hook to one of the gliders. Relieved of the weight, you can then let the whole curtain drop gently towards the floor and get on with matching curtain hooks to gliders so that the curtain is properly hung. Work backwards from the crossover arm towards the window edge. If there are too many gliders for the number of hooks you have used, push the surplus ones to the end of the track and store a few of them there, removing the excess via the little locking mechanism which most tracks have.

Hang all the curtains in the room and, before you do anything more, you will have to dress them. First you may have to use a steam brush to get travel-creasing out. To dress curtains, pull them fully open and pull the heading between each glider forward so that the material begins to fall in equi-distant folds. Use a strip of clear plastic (cut from the packaging) to tie the folds in position at the top of the curtain – be sure that the leading edge faces towards the window and that it is about 15 cm (6 in) wide. Use these first 'pull forwards' as the guide for pleating down the rest of the curtain, holding the folds in place with strips of clear plastic as you go along.

Sometimes you can find a repeat motif to the pattern which also helps to keep the folds straight. The folds should be about 15 cm (6 in) deep – this is roughly the depth of your fingers and part of the palm of your hand. Do not tie the ties too tightly. Steam between the folds, once they are tied, to set the pleats.

Ask your client to leave the ties in place for several days to allow the curtains to settle down.

Positioning for tie-backs is best done before you dress the curtains. A hole, or holes, must be drilled and reinforced with a plastic plug and the tie-back hook screwed into place.

TIP
Tools like hammers and staple guns will make marks on ceilings and walls however carefully they are used unless they are wrapped or covered in material. Also, remove any finger rings, as gold will leave lines like pencil marks.

▶ A dormer window is easily dressed with hinged tracks on to which the curtains are suspended by a frilled casing; but face fabric must be used on both sides of the curtains.

SUSPENDING PELMETS

The method of suspension for the pelmet will have been decided already. Velcro, plus some carefully hammered-in brass panel pins, will suspend most simple soft pelmets.

You will really need help to install a largish hard pelmet because it is heavy, long and unwieldy. If you have to work single-handed, loop an offcut around the pelmet and hang the pelmet by the loop from a temporary hook in the pelmet board. Once semi-suspended, you will be able to nail it up.

Fix swags and tails with a staple gun and staples. Face-fixing swags and tails is very difficult indeed and has to be done from underneath – avoid this if at all possible. Bay windows often present this problem because the boards for the track have been fixed to the ceiling. If a major redecoration job has been going on, it is worth asking the client to reorganize the tracking, so that you can take the fixings down, dress them, and put them back up again.

Clean, tidy and rearrange the furniture in the room as best you can before leaving a hanging job. Your client will appreciate such thoughtfulness.

MAKING POCKETS FOR STORING HEADING TAPE-STRINGS

You will need a lining offcut which matches the lining of the curtain. It should be about 15 cm (6 in) wide and one of the edges should have a selvage.

Make up a template the size you want the pocket to be and fold the strip of lining as shown in Fig. 101 (a). Do the machining in a continuous operation until you have made sufficient pockets to cater for the job in hand. See Fig. 101 (b).

Fig. 101

▷ (a) Fold the strip of lining offcut to the three quarter mark. Starting at A, machine until you have made enough pockets for the job in hand. Cut apart and turn out.

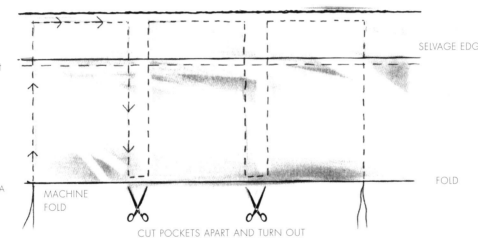

SELVAGE EDGE

FOLD

A

MACHINE FOLD

CUT POCKETS APART AND TURN OUT

▷ (b) Tuck the flap of the pocket under the heading tape at the window edge and machine into place at the same time as you apply the tape.

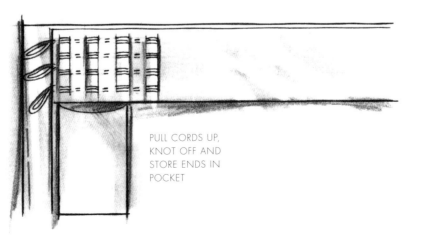

PULL CORDS UP, KNOT OFF AND STORE ENDS IN POCKET

— BASIC SYSTEMS FOR SUSPENSION —

The diagrams show the different basic systems for hanging curtains. Always use specialist designed brackets and pulleys. Look through wholesalers' catalogues to see what is available.

Of course, you charge the client for all the materials which you buy and supply on his or her behalf, putting your own mark up on to the wholesale price.

The large department stores will give you a fair guide to retail pricing of materials such as brackets, tracks and pulleys. Charge for assembly either by the hour or by a flat fee.

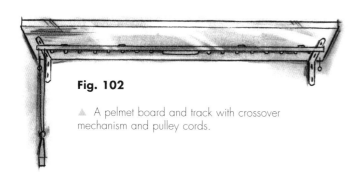

Fig. 102

▲ A pelmet board and track with crossover mechanism and pulley cords.

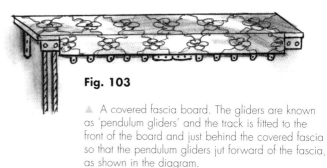

Fig. 103

▲ A covered fascia board. The gliders are known as 'pendulum gliders' and the track is fitted to the front of the board and just behind the covered fascia so that the pendulum gliders jut forward of the fascia, as shown in the diagram.

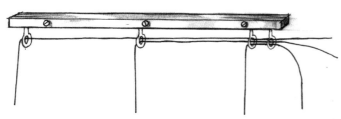

Fig. 104

▲ A simple batten, face or top-fixed, for Austrian and Roman blinds. The eyelet screws should be installed to be on line with the lines of rings at the back of the blind. All the cords are threaded through the last eyelet screw.

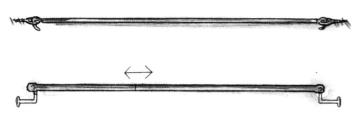

Fig. 105

▲ Poles can be equipped with rings which means that the curtains must be pulled by hand, or the poles can be fitted with integral tracks and pulleys. They are made of metal with various finishes such as brass or wood stained to different colours. The finials are often very beautiful and at the top end of the market poles can be very expensive indeed.

Fig. 106

▲ Either an expanding wire with a hook and eye or a rigid expanding rod can be used to suspend net curtains.

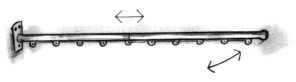

Fig. 107

▲ A hinged track for dormer windows. Such tracks are usually expandable. The curtains must be made of face fabric on both sides as these tracks open and close like cupboard doors.

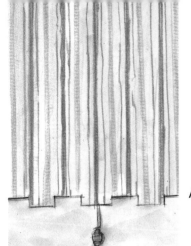

10

MAKING AND HANGING BLINDS

There are three main types of blind: roller, Austrian and Roman.

ROLLER BLINDS

These are made of stiffened fabric or plastic and fixed to the rod with a spring mechanism. They can be bought ready-made or can be made up in your own fabric by firms specializing in this type of work. Special solutions are available to stiffen fabric but the results can be unpredictable, so it is better done by a subcontractor.

Roller blinds with a spring mechanism can prove tricky to keep rolled. A 'bead necklace' pulley mechanism works better in the long term.

AUSTRIAN BLINDS

Two layers of material are made up to form a 'bag' two and a quarter times the width of the window and up to 50 cm (20 in) longer. Austrian blinds have their limitations, despite their popularity, because they are difficult to pull up into attractive folds without spending time primping the folds into

position each time they are adjusted. They are not therefore really suitable for use as a curtain but are fine if not intended to be raised or lowered frequently.

Heavily glazed or thick fabric will not drape properly. As Austrian blinds are 'feminine', they look well trimmed with frilling at sides and base. Without frilling, the strings tend to show at the sides and, even with frilling, the first line of rings should be applied 5–7 cm (2–2¾ in) *in* from the side seams and *up* from the base seam. It is this positioning that makes Austrian blinds drape properly. The rings should be 15 cm (6 in) apart. Using specialist tape or ring tape is hazardous because, unless very carefully applied to ensure that the weft and warp of the weaves are aligned on all three layers, the hang of the blind will distort.

Special tracks are available to suspend Austrian blinds. They, too, have their limitations because light can show through at the top which is not attractive. A simple batten with eyelet screws works well. The suspension can be Velcro, using either the integral

Velcro heading tape or brass panel pins carefully hammered into place through the heading tape.

A pole covered with face fabric and sewn to the back of the Austrian blind, on line with the lowest row of rings, *after* the blind has been put up and dressed, will help to keep it in shape and assist with the raising and lowering.

ROMAN BLINDS

At its simplest a Roman blind is a bag of material, with a batten at the bottom, several rows of sewn-on rings and cords through the rings to make it pull up and down into soft folds. But this basic construction makes a blind that looks amateur. A properly made Roman blind has struts made of thin wood dowelling or, even better, fibreglass dowelling. There are a number of methods to make up Roman blinds. Two reliable ones are described in this chapter.

Roman blinds are suspended in the same way as Austrian blinds, see Fig. 109 (b) and Fig. 111 on pages 136 and 138.

MAKING UP – TAPE-CASING METHOD

Face fabric and lining are cut to the same size. You will need the length and the width plus 2 cm (¾ in) seam

allowance on sides and base. Allow 25–30 cm (10–12 in) extra at the top. Mark the tops with notches. If the

material is patterned, make sure that it is centred and lined up with, say, the curtains at another window.

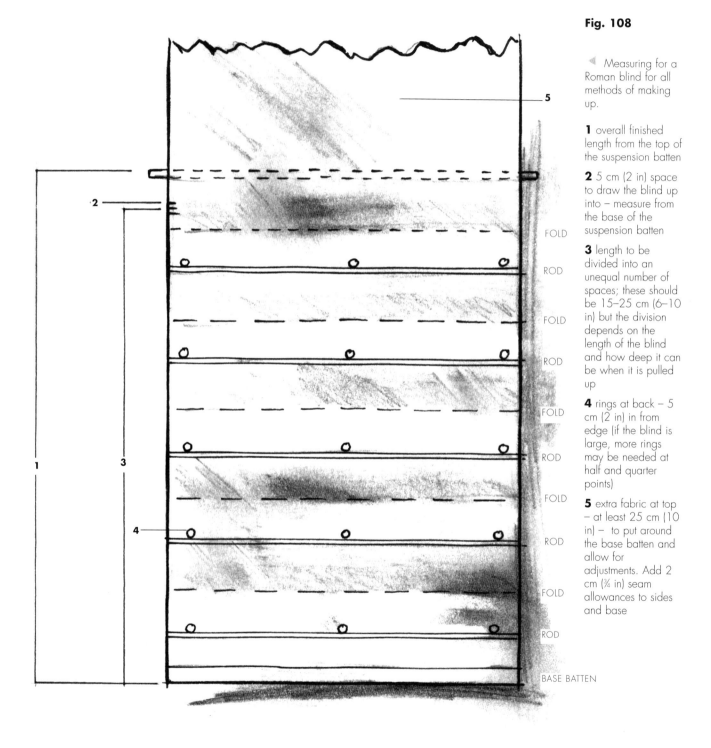

Fig. 108

◀ Measuring for a Roman blind for all methods of making up.

1 overall finished length from the top of the suspension batten

2 5 cm (2 in) space to draw the blind up into – measure from the base of the suspension batten

3 length to be divided into an unequal number of spaces; these should be 15–25 cm (6–10 in) but the division depends on the length of the blind and how deep it can be when it is pulled up

4 rings at back – 5 cm (2 in) in from edge (if the blind is large, more rings may be needed at half and quarter points)

5 extra fabric at top – at least 25 cm (10 in) – to put around the base batten and allow for adjustments. Add 2 cm (¾ in) seam allowances to sides and base

On the lining, with the wrong side facing, iron lines in place to mark the lines for the rods. It is only necessary to iron in those lines which are to have rods. Do not use pencil to mark the lines as it would show through the lining.

Use densely woven India Tape 1.5–2 cm (⅝–¾ in) wide (the former is preferable, but it depends on the thickness of the dowelling used for the rod) and straddle the tape equally down the centre of the ironed marking lines. It is not necessary to pin if you work carefully. Machine in place, using the standard, straight stitch foot on your machine, but first see Fig. 109 (a).

Leaving the top open, machine the sides and base together using a shorter machine stitch than usual.

Iron the seams open and then trim them to 1 cm (⅜ in). Turn inside out and iron so that the lining does not show at the front.

Measure the base batten, remembering to make an allowance for its thickness as well as its width, and 'scratch' a line with a strong needle to mark the stitching line. Pin so that the layers do not travel. Leave long tails of thread and machine along the marked line.

Cut the required number of rods to be 1 cm (⅜ in) shorter than the finished width of the blind. Sandpaper the ends of the rods to smooth and round them. Work your way into the blind until you find the folded open end of the tape at the bottom, and insert a dowel down the casing. Continue inserting rods into all the casings, carefully working them all into place and adjusting them so that there is no tension in the side seams of the blind.

Fig. 109

▽ (a) When you reach about 4 cm (1½ in) from the end, cut the tape off to be on line with the seam allowance of the blind and then fold it back to create a 'hole' 1 cm (⅜ in) in from the seam allowance line. This is the first step towards making a hole into which you will insert a rod. Repeat this step down the other side of the tape.

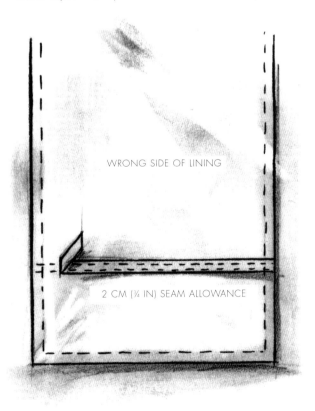

WRONG SIDE OF LINING

2 CM (¾ IN) SEAM ALLOWANCE

▽ (b) Suspend on a face or top fixed 2 x 2 cm (¾ x ¾ in) batten as in the diagram, and also see page 137. Have the pull-up side to the most convenient side for access. If the pull-up side is put behind a large piece of furniture, it will be difficult to reach.

STAPLE

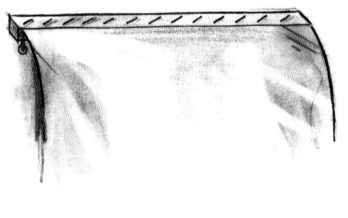

Cut the base batten (a length of lightweight Ramin wood about 5 mm (³⁄₁₆ in) thick and 3–4 cm (1³⁄₁₆–1½ in) wide) to be 1.5 cm (⅝ in) shorter than the finished width of the blind. Sandpaper the ends to smooth and round them.

Use a stitch ripper to open one side of the base batten casing and insert the batten carefully, making sure that the seams are to the back of the batten. Use the long threads to resew the hole, and knot off the long threads at the other end too.

Attach plastic rings to the lining fabric at the back in the positions marked on Fig. 108. If the blind is very large, have sufficient rows of rings to enable the blind to lift and drop comfortably.

As you sew the rings in place, use the thread to catch the face fabric just once to hold the two layers together.

MAKING UP – EXTERIOR-CASING METHOD

For this method, the fabric and the lining are cut to slightly different lengths. Cut the face fabric as described on page 134. Add 2 cm (¾ in) extra per rod to the required length of the lining.

Work out the rod/fold measurements for the blind on a strip of paper, using the diagram instructions as your guide. The fold measurements will remain constant, but the spaces between them, on the rod lines, will be 2 cm (¾ in) width – this is to make the exterior casings for the struts. The lining section will therefore be somewhat longer than the face fabric section at this stage. Fold and iron the 2 cm (¾ in) spaces down their centres right side up. Machine, at 1 cm (⅜ in), along the fold from side to side.

Snip the fold at each end, very

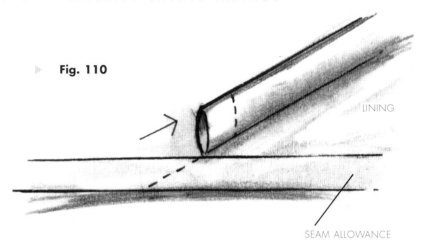

Fig. 110

LINING

SEAM ALLOWANCE

carefully, above the machine stitching and just within the seam allowance. Poke the resulting flap back down the fold. See Fig. 110.

Make sure that the exterior casing is kept away from the machining and make up the rest of the blind as in the previous method.

HANGING AND STRINGING ROMAN AND AUSTRIAN BLINDS

Fig. 104 (page 133) shows the simple type of wooden batten and rings upon which Roman and Austrian blinds can best be suspended. There are, also, sophisticated tracks with inset hook Velcro and purpose-made rings, but these are expensive and also let the light in at the top unless they are installed right against the ceiling.

You can use Velcro to suspend a Roman blind. Position the Velcro so that the adhesive hook length is to the

top of the batten, and machine the loop length above the finished length line of the blind. Alternatively, cut away the excess fabric allowance to give yourself sufficient material to fold under so that you can staple the blind to the top of the batten.

Austrian blinds with pencil pleat tape headings are easy to suspend if you use a press-and-drape heading tape and adhesive Velcro fixed to the batten. For Austrian blinds with triple

French pleat headings, the Velcro must be applied by hand to the back behind the pleats.

To string all types of blind, you will need to position a ladder so that it is square to the window with the rungs facing into the room. Position and fix the blind to the batten. Put a reel of nylon cord into the pocket of your work apron and thread the free end through the hole at the bottom of the pocket. Pull the cord out through the hole as you work, which is a safe way of doing this job.

Bring the blind up and over your head so that you are behind it and make sure that all the rings are in line with the eyelet screws in the batten. Start with the line of rings furthest away from the pulley point (the double eyelet screws) and thread the nylon cord, from the bottom ring upwards, towards the first eyelet screw.

Thread the cord through all the eyelet screws. Cut the cord to leave a generous amount at the pulley end.

Then return to cut and knot the cord to the baseline ring, see Figs. 111 (a) and (b). This type of knot will never come undone and the looping will also hide the cut end which makes it very neat. Start with the first tie of a simple granny knot, then continue making a granny knot but keeping

everything loose enough to turn the cut end of the cord three times round the loop. Pull up firmly and then cut the excess cord off.

Test the blind to ensure that it pulls up evenly and smoothly, adjusting the cords if necessary. A brass cleat screwed to the side of the window is used to secure the cords when the blind is pulled up. Neaten the ends of the cord by putting them into an 'acorn'.

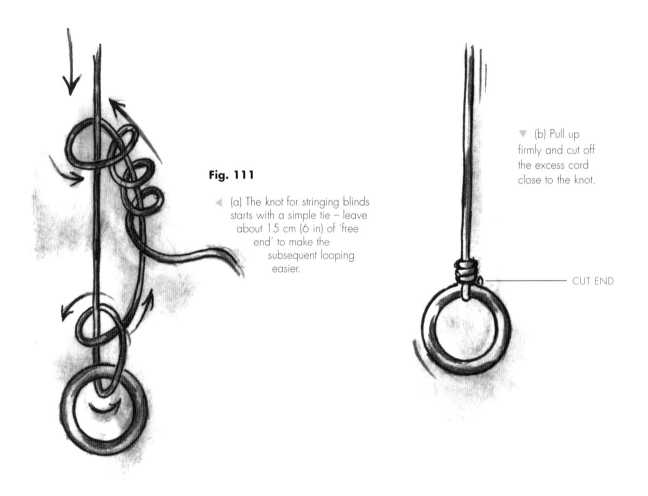

Fig. 111

◀ (a) The knot for stringing blinds starts with a simple tie – leave about 15 cm (6 in) of 'free end' to make the subsequent looping easier.

▼ (b) Pull up firmly and cut off the excess cord close to the knot.

—————— CUT END

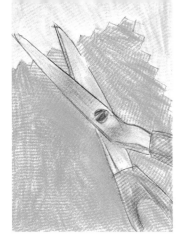

11

CURTAINING
FOR BEDS

Dressing a bed with curtains adds luxury and drama to the room. This treatment does not have to be frilly and 'feminine' – it looks just as good if the curtains are suspended behind a 'masculine' hard pelmet.

▼ A very simple draped canopy above the bed is given a touch of colour with a contrasting fringe and tassels.

TESTER TYPE OF TREATMENT

The pelmet board needs to be wider than usual – 25–30 cm (10–12 in) – and it must be particularly well installed because to be hit on the head by a falling board in the middle of the night would be most unpleasant! The 'L' brackets are screwed in place before the board is put up so that the whole of the underneath of the board can be covered with wadding and the chosen contrast interior fabric stapled into place, tidily, on to the underside of the board. It is necessary to cover the board in this way because it can be seen from underneath by the occupants of the bed.

It is also necessary to finish the job properly by covering the raw edges and staples with a length of lining cut and folded to fit the top and stapled into place. The curtains are suspended from a series of small eyelet screws placed at 5 cm (2 in) intervals around the edge of the board at the back and sides and about 10 cm (4 in) in on either side of the front edge, see Fig. 112 (a).

For this tester treatment the side curtains should be measured, made and hung in the usual way – only one width of fabric is needed for each side curtain. See Fig. 112 (b). The drop for the back curtain, which is separate from the side curtains, is slightly short-er and made up in a slightly different way from a normal lined-only curtain.

This is because the back curtain will hang better if the usual hem is replaced with a casing through which a suitable length of expanding wire can be inserted and fixed to the skirting board with a pair of small hooks. The spaces between the three curtains will enable you to install a brass hold-back or a tie-back to give the side curtains an attractive drape.

The pelmet is suspended in the same way as you would hang any pelmet depending on its style, but it too must be

lined in the same contrasting fabric so that the interior looks good when viewed from below.

Fig. 112

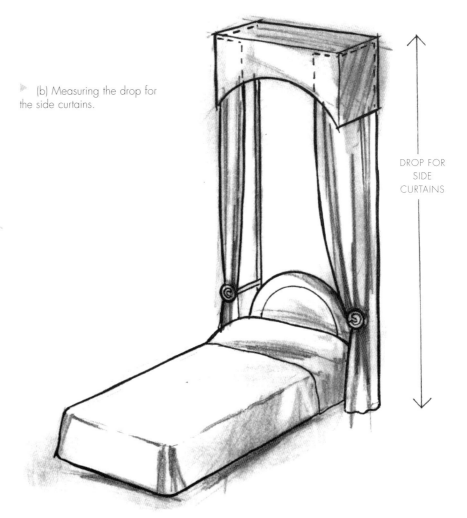

▼ (a) Preparing the pelmet board for a tester.

WIDTH OF BED PLUS 20 CM (8 IN)

COVER THE BOARD WITH WADDING AND CONTRAST FABRIC

SMALL EYELET SCREWS AT 5 CM (2 IN) INTERVALS

25–30 CM (10–12 IN)

▶ (b) Measuring the drop for the side curtains.

DROP FOR SIDE CURTAINS

CORONA TYPE OF TREATMENT

The pelmet board is D-shaped and about 50–60 cm (20–24 in) long at the back and 25–30 cm (10–12 in) deep at the centre of the curve, see Fig. 113 (a). The brackets are placed as for a tester, and covered with wadding and fabric. The eyelet screws are put in all round the shape at intervals of 5 cm (2 in) and the side curtains should cross over one another a little bit at the front.

The side curtains are hooked up at about the level of the corner of the headboard to give them a graceful curve, and it is this measurement which will be the length of the curtain. As always, it is safest to take this measurement after the board has been installed. Use a length of string pinned to the front of the board and looped back towards the wall at a point just above the corner of the headboard, see Fig. 113 (b).

A measurement taken from this point will give you an excess of fabric at floor level towards the back of the drape when the curtain is hung and arranged. This is fine if you want the opulent look of fabric lying on the floor but if not, take a second measurement from the back of the board to the floor and make the curtain up with a hem angled between these two measurements. It does, however, look attractive to make the side curtains up to the back measurement because the 'shortening' which will happen at the front when the curtain is hung and draped, will fold

Fig. 113

▽ (a) A corona is D-shaped and large enough to accommodate three to four widths of fabric underneath it.

▷ (b) It is best to install the corona board before taking measurements for the side curtains.

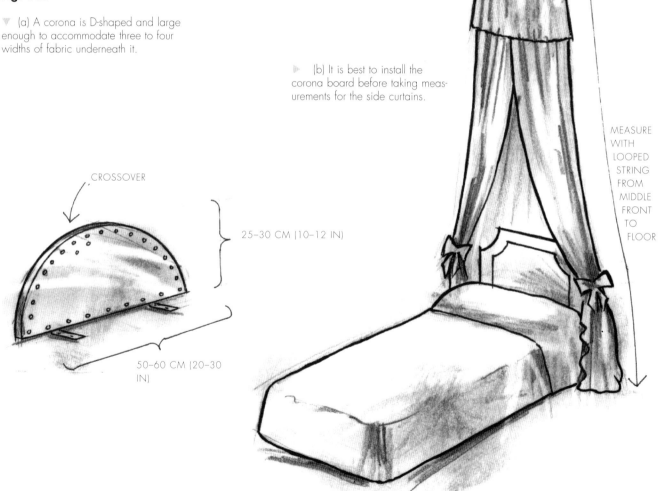

CROSSOVER

25–30 CM (10–12 IN)

50–60 CM (20–30 IN)

MEASURE WITH LOOPED STRING FROM MIDDLE FRONT TO FLOOR

like a tail to show the contrast fabric.

The back curtain requires a tent shape to make it hang well, see Fig. 113 (c). This can be achieved by adding a 'wedge' of face fabric on each side so that there is greater fullness at the cased hem than there is at the heading. Once again, securing the base of the back curtain with an expanding wire will make it look very neat, though it will rise to an arc shape in the middle but this is hidden by the head-board.

As with the pelmet for the tester style, the pelmet for a corona style will have to be put up in a way that suits what you have chosen to make. For a first effort it might be a good idea to have a small, straight gathered pelmet headed on to press-'n'-drape tape – but do not forget that the lining must match the interior of the whole canopy.

Another method of creating a canopy above a bed can be achieved with poles and brackets designed to stick straight out from the wall. These poles can be bought, as kits, from most good track suppliers and they are also available through wholesalers.

The pole must be attached to the wall fairly high up above the bed – if it is low, it will look squat and heavy and the whole effect will be lost. To decide what height would look best, pin a length of cord above the bed at the centre point and then drape the cord towards the side of the bed to see what the curve looks like. Adjust the height and the cord until you are satisfied.

The length of the cord, to the floor, will be the length required for the drapes from the top of the pole down-wards, but remember that there is a little bit of take up round the pole when the material is cased on to it.

The two drapes can be simply made as a 'bag' of face and contrast fabric, with the top turned to create a frill which, when added to the frill on the opposite drape and sewn together to make a casing for the pole, is very pretty. The drapes simply have to be arranged on the shorter side-arm poles.

It is not necessary to make a back curtain (which is why this treatment is popular) but the look of the interior of the canopy will be enhanced by an appropriate picture hung in the space.

Fig. 113 (continued)

▶ (c) The back drop needs to be pulled up very tightly to make the tent shape fall gracefully.

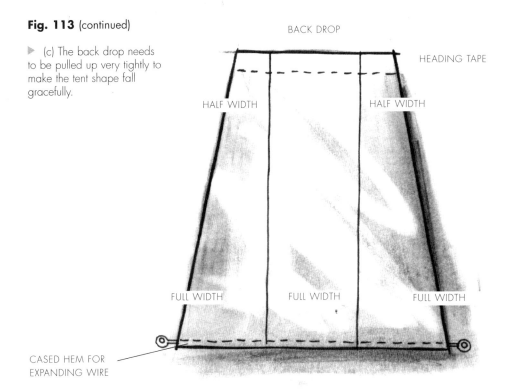

BACK DROP

HEADING TAPE

HALF WIDTH   HALF WIDTH

FULL WIDTH   FULL WIDTH   FULL WIDTH

CASED HEM FOR
EXPANDING WIRE

▶ A 'sunburst' effect, as used in the ends of bolsters, looks equally attractive on a round cushion.

12
CUSHIONS

C ushions are highly decorative items with an infinite number of shapes, colours, fabrics and trimmings. For instance, I have seen them made of knitted chenille with a toning tassel, of patchwork of greater and lesser degrees of sophistication, of silken embroidery, of woven velvet ribbons, and some with Valentine and other messages.

In addition to your photographs of window treatments, it is also a good idea to collect illustrations of cushions.

MAKING A CUSHION COVER

Making a cushion cover embodies a number of techniques which are used in other branches of soft furnishing.

You will need to make, and keep, a series of templates for making cushions, so that you do not need to measure up and mark out every time, see Fig. 114. These templates should be squares measuring 34 cm (13⅜ in), 40 cm (15¾ in), 45 cm (17¾ in), 50 cm (19¾ in) and 55 cm (21⅝ in). These measurements include seam allowances of 2 cm (¾ in) and will give you the right size cover to take 30 cm (11¹³⁄₁₆ in), 36 cm (14⅛ in), 41 cm (16⅛ in), 46 cm (18⅛ in) and 51 cm (20¹⁄₁₆ in) pads. You should use a size larger pad and overstuff the cover initially because it only takes a month or two for the stuffing to break down and soften, after which the cushion will be perfect.

The templates should also be marked with the length of piping cord, bias strip and frilling that each size will require. This will save you hours of time calculating. Notch the seam allowances, as shown in Figs. 114 and 115 (a), so that you can get the different sections sewn together the right way round and up.

Circular cushions need templates for both the fronts and the backs, see Fig. 115 (a). It is not possible to insert a zip neatly on a curve so place the zip in a straight line across the centre of the back of the circular cushions, with the template positioned to ensure that the fabric pattern will be complete when the zip is put in, see Fig. 115 (b).

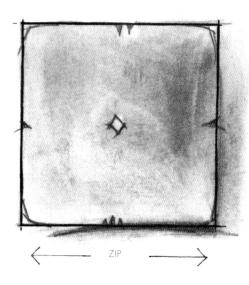

ZIP

Fig. 114

▲ (a) The templates should be pared at the corners, and also have a peep-hole in the middle so that centring a design is easier. Always choose a section of the fabric pattern which will look attractive when seen in the 'frame' of a cushion and, if making several cushions, they should all match both on the front and the back.

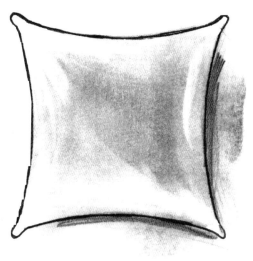

▲ (b) If the corners of cushion squares are not pared, the end product will have pointed 'ears' – an unattractive fault.

T I P

If you are using a lightweight or pure silk fabric, you should back it with a pre-shrunk calico or lining material. It will machine up much better.
Patchwork or strips of material joined to make an interesting face to a cushion must be reinforced with backing material. There would be too much strain on the seams otherwise.

Circular cushions, even when frilled, usually have a dimpled look round the piped edges but this cannot be avoided.

STUFFING AND PADDING FOR CUSHIONS

Cushion pads come in standard sizes and are available from wholesalers at a much lower price than in the shops. Mark up the wholesale price to the current retail rate. Unless you want a particularly unusual shape, it is not worth making up your own cushion pads. Some suppliers will make up special shapes if you provide them with a template; the cost is very little more than for an ordinary pad.

Feathers are the best stuffing for cushions. Check that they have been sterilized and that the quality is such that there are no quill feathers or hard bits in the mixture. The best covering for feather pads is waxed cambric, with the waxed side used inside. Feathers work their way out of unwaxed fabric very quickly.

The second best stuffing for cushions is kapok. It is rather heavy and solid, and has a lifespan of about two years before it breaks down totally and turns into little lumps.

Polyester wadding makes a reasonable stuffing but it flattens and goes hard and lumpy quite quickly. Foam chips are very unsatisfactory.

Polyester foam/sponge varies in density and is used for squab cushions, welted cushions and bolsters. You probably can buy the necessary cylinder shape through a wholesaler. It should be covered with soft 50–100g (2–4oz) polyester wadding and a further cover made of pre-shrunk calico, lining material or stockinette (which is available in tubular form from some suppliers).

FASTENINGS AND OPENINGS FOR CUSHIONS

The best opening/closing for a cushion is a seam, ladder-stitched (see mitres, page 47) by hand. For this type of opening the raw edges of the seam should be zigzagged and a line of stitches also machined along the seam line to act as reinforcement and a guideline for the ladder stitching. But only people with needlework skills will appreciate this sort of opening; it is tedious to remove and replace the cover for cleaning.

The most practical and neatest closure is a zip. Use strong dressmaking zips in a colour which will match the main fabric and buy them in bulk in a wide variety of colours in 50 cm (20 in) lengths which can be cut back and oversewn to the required size. Zipping is also available in continuous lengths with locks which you apply yourself. This type of zip should be used on welted cushions, because it is very much stronger, but applying the locks is not easy – the supplier may be willling to do this for you.

Zips are fiddly to insert into a piped cushion and it requires practice and patience to perfect the method so that you can cut, pipe, zip, machine and trim a simple cushion cover quickly.

Hooks, snap fasteners and ready-made snap fasteners on a tape look dreadful when the seam gapes open. Do not use any of these for cushions but ready-made snaps are acceptable for duvet covers (which are really also a type of cushion cover!). Velcro is unsuitable for cushion covers.

Fig. 115

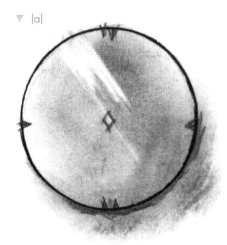

▼ (a)

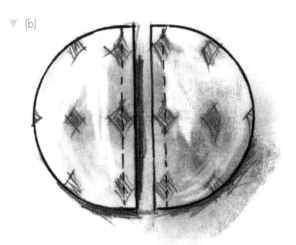

▼ (b)

▲ Cushions lend themselves to endless decorative variation. Leather and tweed are a classic combination and look good on studded leather armchairs.

MAKING A SIMPLE CUSHION
COVER WITH PIPING AND A ZIP

Fig. 116

Measure the cushion pad and use the appropriate size template. Cut out the face fabric and bias strip for piping. Join the bias strips.

Zigzag the raw edge of the back section of the face fabric on the three-notch edge, see Fig. 116 (a).

Apply the bias strip and cord to the right side of the front section of the face fabric, starting at the three-notch edge and using the method described on page 84. See Fig. 116 (b).

Match the notches on the front (piped) and back (zigzagged) sections. Change to a zip foot. With the piped section (the one for the zip) upper most and using the machine stitching as a guide, machine 4 cm (1⅝ in) down from the top and then reverse the stitching to reinforce, see Fig. 116 (c). Do the same at the other end. This will give you an 'open book' with a hole in the spine!

Make sure the zip (marked 'A' in diagram) is face down and pin the flap at the top in position so that the 'stop' for the lock is about 1 cm (⅜ in) above the end of the 4 cm (1⅝ in) of stitching. Open the zip to its full extent, see Fig. 116 (d).

▲ (a)

RIGHT SIDE BACK

RIGHT SIDE FRONT

▲ (b)

Keeping the unpiped side of the seam well out of the way, pack the teeth of the open zip carefully against the piping and machine as close as possible to the teeth and right to the end of the cover. Close the zip, making absolutely sure that the lock is in the open position. You will be in dire trouble later on if you do not do this!

Tack the unpiped side of the seam, along the seam allowance line, down between the teeth of the zip and the piping, see Fig. 116 (e). It is best to do this with a trailing knot at one end and not knotted off at the other, so that the tacking thread can be removed easily. Turn the 'book' to the right side.

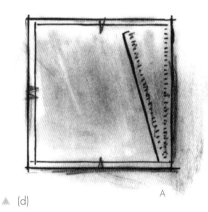

▲ (d)

A

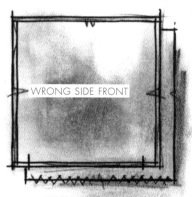

WRONG SIDE FRONT

MACHINE 4 CM (1⅜ IN) TO
MAKE 'BOOK' WITH OPEN SPINE

▲ (c)

WRONG SIDE OF
UNPIPED SIDE

▲ (e)

WARNING

If you are using any type of polyester foam/sponge as the stuffing for cushions you must (by law) ensure that it is fireproofed.

Fig. 116 (continued)

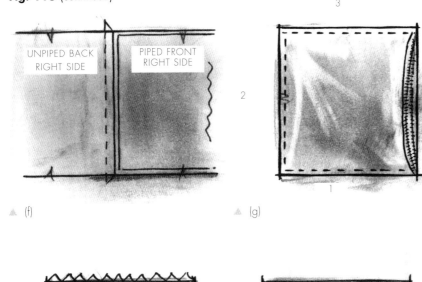

(f)

(g)

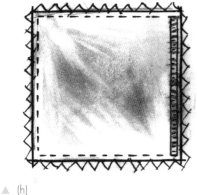

(h)

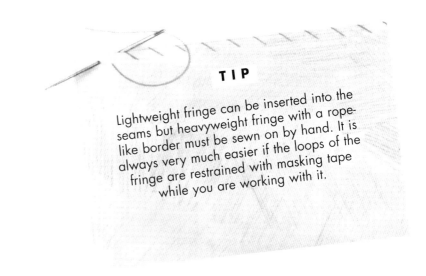

(i)

'open book' with a slight hole in the spine!

With the piped section and wrong side uppermost, pin the two sections together, matching notches, see Fig. 116 (g). Ensure that the raw edges of the piping have not turned back into the seam at the corners. Continue to use the zip-foot and the previous machine stitching as a guide, and making sure that the seam around the zip is lying flat and true, machine all three remaining sides of the cover.

Remove the pins. Open the zip completely, turn the cover inside out to check everything from the right side. If all is well turn it back again, trim the seams to 1.5 cm (⅝ in) and zigzag all round, see Fig. 116 (h).

Press the cover and insert a cushion pad, making sure that the corners are well stuffed up into the corners of the cover, see Fig. 116 (i).

Tack the second side of the zip to the unpiped side of the seam, using the teeth as the tacking guide and stitching close to the teeth, see Fig. 116 (f). Taking great care to keep the machine stitching straight as you pass the lock of the zip and with the right side of the fabric uppermost, machine stitch the zip into position. The stitching should be just a tiny bit away from the line of tacking and go from top to bottom of the section. Remove all the tacking and push the lock of the zip down so that the zip is slightly open. (Failure to do this will also get you into dire trouble later on!) At this point you have an

TIP

Lightweight fringe can be inserted into the seams but heavyweight fringe with a rope-like border must be sewn on by hand. It is always very much easier if the loops of the fringe are restrained with masking tape while you are working with it.

──── FRILLED CUSHIONS ────

Attaching frilling round a cushion adds to the work and, therefore, to the cost of producing it. On pages 97–105 several methods for making up frilling to achieve differing effects are given with quick and simple ways of gathering and applying the frilling.

For cushions the frilling must be joined to form a circle twice the total length of the sides of the cushion – for example, a 51 cm (20¹⁄₁₆ in) square cushion will need 4.08 m (160 in) of frilling. With some styles of frilling, such as Type 2 (page 103), it is not very easy to rejoin the three different layers of fabric. I usually unpick a section of the seam at both ends of the made-up frill and rejoin each part separately to form the circle, then press the joins flat and machine across the resulting gap to close it. Apply zigzag gathering at the 1 cm (⅜ in) mark, see Fig. 117 (a). Put

pins to indicate the quarter-mark sections of the frill.

If the frilled cushion has no piping, it is not difficult to pull up the gathering and to dispose it evenly around the cushion. Apply the frilling to the top section of the cover, see Fig. 117 (b). The frilling will lie more easily at the corners if the seam allowance and the zigzag are snipped through by 1.5 cm (⅝ in) so that the gathering opens out to be flat as it turns the corner. Push a little extra gathering towards the corners on both sides to help the frill to look full over these points. Make sure that the raw edge of the frilling lies accurately along the raw edge of the cushion cover and insert the pins so that they are well back from the sewing line. It is helpful to iron the raw edge of the frilling, within the seam allowance, as this helps everything

to lie flat. It is also a good idea to secure the frilling with masking tape while you are working on it to make sure that the gathering remains upright.

The same method of applying frilling should be used if the cushion cover is piped, but if at all possible try to apply the piping and the frilling in one operation to avoid the puckering effect which happens with too many lines of machine stitching. If the piping is tacked in place (use matching thread), it is quite easy to use the cording foot to machine both the piping and frill down at the same time. This can be done with a zip foot but you have to be very much more careful. Once the piping and the frill are in place, following the instructions on page 147 from the point when the flap of the zip is pinned in position.

Fig. 117

(a) Preparing the frill for a cushion.

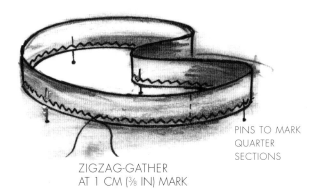

ZIGZAG-GATHER
AT 1 CM (⅜ IN) MARK

PINS TO MARK
QUARTER
SECTIONS

(b) Attaching the frill to the top section of the cushion cover.

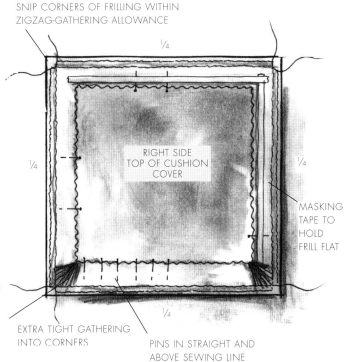

SNIP CORNERS OF FRILLING WITHIN
ZIGZAG-GATHERING ALLOWANCE

¼

¼

RIGHT SIDE
TOP OF CUSHION
COVER

¼

MASKING
TAPE TO
HOLD
FRILL FLAT

EXTRA TIGHT GATHERING
INTO CORNERS

PINS IN STRAIGHT AND
ABOVE SEWING LINE

¼

▲ Soft furnishing is not confined to the house. Here a garden sofa has been made comfortable with sunburst bolsters, finished with tassels.

———— WELTED CUSHIONS ————

These are the kind of cushions you find on sofas. They have a sort of 'wall' (the welt) between two lines of piping, and the zip is inserted on a separately made-up section of the welt in the back of the cushion. Make sure that the zip (use heavy-duty continuous zipping) is long enough to go a little way around the sides of the cushion which is usually stiff and bulky and therefore difficult to get into the cover

if the zip is too short. The zip should be concealed under a flap of folded fabric (as is the zip in a dress or skirt) and constructed so that the pattern matches.

If the fabric is suitable, the welt should also pattern-match the top of the cover along the front edge but it is, of course, almost impossible to pattern-match along the sides. Try to avoid having any seams in the welt along the

front edge, though this is not possible if the cushion is very long.

It is necessary to make a template for this type of cushion if the shape is complicated. You can make one from face fabric pinned to the cushion itself and then use the resulting template, with seam allowances added, (with the fabric placed wrong side to wrong side) to pattern-match and cut the lower section. Work out the cutting of the welt so that the pattern will match the top of the cushion at the front. See Fig. 118 (a).

Apply piping round both the top and bottom sections, then centre and pattern-match the welt around the top section, snipping at the corners to help the welt to lie well. For accuracy it is best to tack the welt in place, especially at the corners. Centre and pattern-match the zip section along the back of the cover, taking it round the corners and joining it to the first welt section so that it fits the cover exactly, see Fig. 118 (b). Use a zip foot or, preferably, a cording foot to machine the welt in place.

◀ A folded frill enhances this plain cushion cover made in a multi-coloured fabric.

Check that the corners are properly sewn before attaching the lower cover to the welt. Open the zip a little before doing this or it will be very difficult to undo the zip to turn the cover inside out. Check the corners of the lower section. Trim the seams to 1 cm (⅜ in) all round and then zigzag the raw edges. Insert the cushion pad, making sure that the seams all face into the welt.

Fig. 118

▼ (a) The top and bottom sections of a welted cushion should be piped to give extra strength.

▼ (b) Position the zip, making sure that the pattern matches.

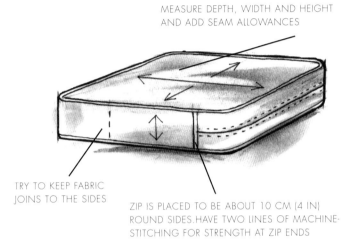

MEASURE DEPTH, WIDTH AND HEIGHT AND ADD SEAM ALLOWANCES

TRY TO KEEP FABRIC JOINS TO THE SIDES

ZIP IS PLACED TO BE ABOUT 10 CM (4 IN) ROUND SIDES. HAVE TWO LINES OF MACHINE-STITCHING FOR STRENGTH AT ZIP ENDS

BOLSTERS

Bolsters are another form of welted, circular cushion and it is useful to know how to make them. Old, deep-sided sofas can be made much more comfortable if bolsters are made for each end so that people can rest their arms at a proper height.

The stuffing for a bolster can be soft, such as feathers, or very firm, such as a cylinder of polyurethane foam (see warning on page 147). Both are available from wholesalers or, on order, from shops specializing in upholstery supplies. If you use a foam cylinder, you will have to make an extra calico or lining cover for it to prevent the outer cover from creeping.

The only real difficulty in making a bolster is the insertion of the zip because the tube is usually long and narrow. It is therefore best to tack the zip in place before machining it, see Fig. 119 (a). Use a zip which is long enough to fit the cylinder from end to end as this will make it very much easier to insert the stiff foam.

Measure the sofa for which the bolster is intended to get the length and then decide the diameter of the circular ends, depending on the use to which the bolster is intended to be put. Add seam allowances to these measurements.

Cut bias strip piping and apply to the circles, see Fig. 119 (b). Fit the zip to the tube made up to fit the cylinder and, if there is a pattern to be kept upright and visible, make sure that the piped circles are fitted so that the zip is at the base of the pattern, see Fig. 119 (c). Machine the circles in place, trim the resulting raw edges and then zigzag.

If you want to have a sunburst-gathered end to the bolster, measure the circumference of the cylinder and make a strip of fabric to that size, with a seam allowance to one side only. Join the strip to form a circle; the depth of the strip will be half the diameter of the circle less 1 cm (⅜ in).

Zigzag gather the inner edge, using a very shallow zigzag, as close to the raw edge as you can. Attach the strip to the outside edge of a circle of calico or lining cut to the same size, plus seam allowances, as the end of the cylinder. Gather up the zigzag gathering tightly and then centre the gathered edge on to the calico/lining circle and sew it in place. Cover the gathering with a large covered button or, for an even more elegant look, with a tassel with a boss. See Fig. 119 (d).

Fig. 119

▼ (a) Make a tube of fabric as shown in the diagram in order to fit the bolster cylinder.

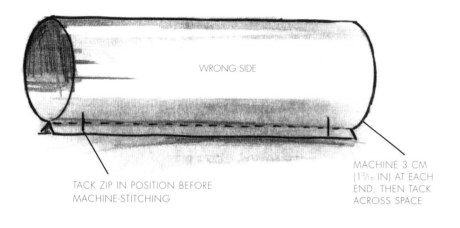

WRONG SIDE

TACK ZIP IN POSITION BEFORE
MACHINE-STITCHING

MACHINE 3 CM
(1³⁄₁₆ IN) AT EACH
END, THEN TACK
ACROSS SPACE

▼ (b) Apply piping to the end circles.

RIGHT SIDE

APPLY PIPING TO END CIRCLES
SNIP EDGE TO MAKE IT LIE FLAT

▼ (c) Placement for zip and end circles.

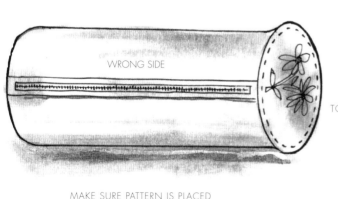

WRONG SIDE

TOP

MAKE SURE PATTERN IS PLACED
TO BE UPRIGHT FROM ZIP

▼ (d) The sunburst is flat round the outer edge and gathered in the centre.

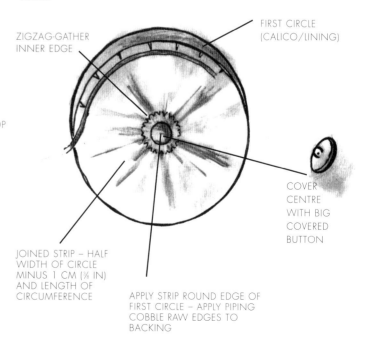

ZIGZAG-GATHER
INNER EDGE

FIRST CIRCLE
(CALICO/LINING)

COVER
CENTRE
WITH BIG
COVERED
BUTTON

JOINED STRIP – HALF
WIDTH OF CIRCLE
MINUS 1 CM (⅜ IN)
AND LENGTH OF
CIRCUMFERENCE

APPLY STRIP ROUND EDGE OF
FIRST CIRCLE – APPLY PIPING
COBBLE RAW EDGES TO
BACKING

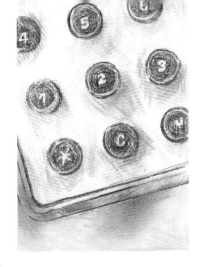

13

RUNNING A BUSINESS FROM HOME

Administration may seem the most tedious aspect of running a business from your own home but it is an integral part. As a self-employed person you are responsible for keeping accurate financial records. Even if you do not think it necessary to employ an accountant to handle your tax returns, it is worth consulting one who specializes in self-employed clients before you start your business. You can then find out, for instance, which expenses are deductible and how best to keep these separate from your own personal expenses.

COSTING YOUR WORK

Find out the going rate for the sort of work you do; this may involve some ingenuity. Do not undercharge as this under-values your hard-earned skills and may also put longer established people out of work.

Costing your work becomes easier if you compile a list of all the different processes involved and decide on appropriate charges for each. You may have other expenses that should be charged to the client such as parking fees, postage and spray starch. Charge a flat fee per window to cover the cost of items such as panel pins and hooks. A sample price list is given . . .

WORKING WITH OTHER PEOPLE

Tempting as it may be to find a companion with whom to share the working hours, do be cautious about going into partnership with someone. There could well be differences of opinion over standards of work as well as money.

If you need sub-contractors or out-workers, make sure your instructions are very clear and keep a copy for your records. By the time you are working seriously, you will have found a competent track fitter. Your wholesale supplier may be able to recommend one. For small jobs you should be able to assemble and install tracks yourself.

BALANCING YOUR TIME

Being self-employed it is very easy to fall into the habit of working excessively long hours. Try to organize your time to maintain a balanced working and social life.

Work regular hours if possible. You will not make a satisfactory profit if you do not discipline yourself to work six to eight hours most days, remembering to take a two-day break every week. Working from home means that you can choose when to work in terms of both the hours of the day and the days of the week. It is a good idea to have an answerphone, especially for times when you are working non-standard hours – otherwise clients might think that you had given up your business.

▶ A lambrequin is a long-sided hard pelmet usually fitted at the front of the reveal. The fixing is 2 x 2 cm (¾ x ¾ in) batten and Velcro.

Sample Price List

Style No. and Item	Description	Trade	Private
1 Curtains (per width and half-width)	Unlined, tape heading, machined sides and hem	£00.00	£00.00
	Lined, tape heading, hand-slipped sides and hem	£00.00	£00.00
	Interlined, tape heading, hand-slipped sides and hem	£00.00	£00.00
	Handmade headings, per pleat	00p	00p

Pricing is for curtains up to 2.5 m (2¾ yd) length. Add £00.00 per each extra 50 cm (20 in) or part thereof to lined curtains. Add £00.00 per each extra 50 cm (20 in) or part thereof to interlined curtains. Add £00.00 per width for silk, velvet, dupion, etc.

Style No. and Item	Description	Trade	Private
2 Tie-Backs to include rings and buckram, all interlined. Priced per tie-back	Plain, simple shape	£00.00	£00.00
	Piped, shaped	£00.00	£00.00
	Frilled – plus cost per m (yd) for type of frill chosen	£00.00	£00.00
	Plaited – soft with reinforced back	£00.00	£00.00
3 Pelmets up to 1 m (yd) drop, per width or part-width	Lined, bag hem, tape heading	£00.00	£00.00
	Interlined, bag hem, tape heading	£00.00	£00.00
	Hand-made headings – as above	£00.00	£00.00
	Shaped – simple, add	£00.00	£00.00
	Shaped – complicated, add	£00.00	£00.00
	Box pleating, per width	£00.00	£00.00
	Buckram band, per m (yd)	£00.00	£00.00
	Ruching on band, per finished m (yd)	£00.00	£00.00
4 Hard Pelmets	Basic price per m (yd) up to 1 m (yd) long	£00.00	£00.00
	Shaped – simple, add	£00.00	£00.00
	Shaped – complicated, add	£00.00	£00.00

Piping, braid, fringe, etc. applied to the above will be charged as per Extras pricing.

Style No. and Item	Description	Trade	Private
5 Swags and Tails	Lined	£00.00	£00.00
	Interlined	£00.00	£00.00

The above are basic prices per each swag and each tail. Piping, braid, fringe, rope etc. applied to the above will be charged as per Extras pricing.

Style No. and Item	Description	Trade	Private
6 Roman blind	Small, up to 1 sq. m (10¾ sq. ft.)	£00.00	£00.00
	Medium, up to 1.5 sq. m (16 sq. ft.)	£00.00	£00.00
	Large, up to 2 sq. m (21½ sq. ft.)	£00.00	£00.00
7 Austrian blind	Lined, per width or part-width. Up to 2.5 m (2¾ yd). Add £00.00 per extra 50 cm (20 in)	£00.00 £00.00	£00.00 £00.00

Frilling, piping, etc. charged as per Extras pricing. Festoons are charged at double the basic price plus price per extra 50 cm (20 in).

Style No. and Item	Description	Trade	Private
8 Tablecloths	As per curtains per width or part-width plus Extras	£00.00	£00.00

SAMPLE PRICE LIST CONT.

Style No. and Item	Description		Trade	Private
9 Bedbase, lined with frame and piping	Gathered:			
	Single		£00.00	£00.00
	Double		£00.00	£00.00
	King		£00.00	£00.00
	Extra large		£00.00	£00.00
	Box pleating – Add £00.00		£00.00	£00.00
10 Cushions, square or round	Plain, zip:	30 cm (13¾ in) square or round	£00.00	£00.00
		40 cm (15¾ in) square or round	£00.00	£00.00
		45 cm (17¾ in) square or round	£00.00	£00.00
		50 cm (19¾ in) square or round	£00.00	£00.00
	Piped, zip – add £00.00 per m (yd) or part thereof to above prices			
11 Extras	Rope, braid and fringe		£00.00	£00.00
	hand-applied, per m (yd)		£00.00	£00.00
	machine-applied, per m (yd)		£00.00	£00.00
	Piping, per m (yd)		£00.00	£00.00
	CONTRAST BINDING:		£00.00	£00.00
	straight-cut, per m (yd)		£00.00	£00.00
	bias-cut, per m (yd)		£00.00	£00.00
	FRILLING, PER FINISHED M (YD)			
	Type one (fold)		£00.00	£00.00
	Type Two		£00.00	£00.00
	Type Three		£00.00	£00.00
	Type Four		£00.00	£00.00
	Type Five		£00.00	£00.00
	ROSETTES AND BOWS			
	From £00.00 upwards. Cost per item will depend upon complexity			
	Hand-gathering £00.00 – £00.00 per width			
	Hand-smocking £00.00 – £00.00 per width			
	Velcro, machine-applied £00.00 per m (yd)			
	Velcro, hand-applied £00.00 per m (yd)			
	Hand-sewn hooks 00p each			

Lining, interlinings, etc. at competitive retail prices. Tracks, poles, etc. will be estimated.
Travel – £00.00 per km (30 miles) or part thereof. Hanging time charged at £00.00 per hour locally – £00.00 per hour otherwise.
Prices subject to change.

Do you see from the above how relatively easy it becomes to collate the prices for making-up charges? Depending on the type of work, you will have other expenses to include such as spray starch, parking fees, postage, tie-back hooks, acorns, cleats, etc. Charge a flat fee per window to cover the cost of hooks, panel pins, etc.

INDEX

Acknowledgements

Photographs from:

p2 Trevor Richards © House & Garden, Conde Nast, p6 Sanderson: 0171 584 3344, p10 Harlequin Fabrics & Furnishings, p23 Houses & Interiors: Simon Butcher, p26 Sanderson: 0171 584 3344, p27l Nursery Window, p27r Harrison Drape, p31t Elizabeth Whiting & Associates, p31b Stiebel of Nottingham, p34 Bo Appeltofft/Camera Press Ltd, p35 Trevor Richards © House & Garden, Conde Nast, p38 Sanderson: 0171 584 3344, p42 Designer pole collection from Swish, p51 Twinglyde track from Swish, pp54–5 Jo Alderson Collection/Harrison Drape, p71 Spike Powell/Elizabeth Whiting & Associates, p74 Albemarle/Design Archives, p75 Dragons of Walton Street, p78 Elizabeth Whiting & Associates, p79 Sanderson: 0171 584 3344, p82 Today Interiors, p83 Paradiso/Osborne & Little, p90 Jo Alderson Collection/Harrison Drape, p95 Dorma Prestige Collection, p99 Today Interiors, p103 Superluxe track from Swish, p111 Houses & Interiors: Simon Butcher, pp118–9 Welbeck Golin/Harris Communications Ltd, pp122–3 Simon Upton/Elizabeth Whiting & Associates, p127 Keith Scott Morton © House & Garden, Conde Nast, p131 Di Lewis/Elizabeth Whiting & Associates, p139 From the *Kingfisher Bedroom Book* by Forbo Lancaster, p143 Homes & Gardens/Robert Harding Syndication, p146 Christopher Drake © House & Garden, Conde Nast, p150 Romo Ltd 01623 756 699, p151 ICI Paints: Welbeck Golin/Harris Communications Ltd, p155 Homes & Gardens/Robert Harding Syndication.